I0814404

PRAISE FOR
WISDOM FROM THE WILD FOR YOUTH

"*Wisdom from the Wild for Youth* is a fierce, funny, and refreshingly honest guide to growing up and leading with heart. By listening to nature, this book speaks volumes about how young people can find their niche in leadership."

—**Christian Greer,** EdD, president and CEO, Michigan Science Center

"This book is a brilliant blend of leadership, storytelling, and awesome animals. Julie, Tasman, and Kepler blend their perspectives to give young leaders an engaging tool to understand important concepts of empathetic and courageous leadership. Interesting, relatable, and full of heart."

—**Katie Gabe,** graduate student, marine biology, College of Charleston

"Having witnessed Julie Henry ignite transformation in both the boardroom and the classroom, I can attest to the profound impact of her leadership principles. I know firsthand the challenge of finding resources that truly resonate with young leaders. After dedicating a summer to crafting a leadership curriculum for my students, I was astounded by the magic that unfolded when Julie Henry stepped into our lecture hall. She engaged teenagers with concepts typically reserved for CEOs in a way no textbook or lesson plan could ever achieve. Now, this remarkable book offers that same transformative experience to a wider audience."

—**Susan Hedgcock,** PhD, department chair at
Sarasota Christian School, College Board AP Reader

"This engaging book is easy to comprehend and connect with. I love all the different areas: Tasman's and Kepler's perspectives, brain breaks, real-life applications, and my favorite—the intriguing quotes. I have heard lots of different lectures about leadership and have always wished I could hear someone talk about confidence while also speaking on empathy and balance. I have been told that I am not a leader in the past, so thank you for mentioning different situations and leadership types I can relate to. I am excited to read this in my college dorm room because no matter how many times I read it, I can always learn something from a book like this."

—high school senior

"I wish I would have had this go-to book on leadership to share with my three children. Julie, Tasman, and Kepler share stories and examples that will truly resonate with youth wanting to build their leadership skills and confidence."

—Heather Kasten, president and CEO,
The Greater Sarasota Chamber of Commerce

"I always thought that a leader had to be outgoing and talkative, but I learned that even though I am not that way at all, I can still be a leader."

—high school junior

"Where was this book when I was an awkward kid trying to find my voice? Full of humor, heart, and unexpected wisdom from nature—from barnacles to bats—it reminds us that real leadership starts with knowing yourself. A refreshing blend of insight and practical advice for young people ready to lead in a way that's true to who they are."

—Rachel Bergren, executive director, Heaven Can Wait Animal Society

"As a fan of *Wisdom from the Wild* and as a mom of teenagers, I was delighted to discover Julie's latest book that centers on youth leadership. *Wisdom from the Wild for Youth* serves as an engaging guide for the younger generation as they embark on their own leadership endeavors."

—Pam Lanter, PT, DPT, MBA, non-profit leader

"This book has truly allowed me to view leadership from a new perspective. While I used to believe that leadership was an innate character trait, I have since learned that anyone can be a leader and that every leader guides in their own way. Using animals to explain leadership was an extremely clever and effective way to connect with a youth audience and take complex, abstract ideas and turn them concrete. By doing this, it created a safe space for the reader—a place to grow, learn, and make mistakes. Ultimately, it created an environment for self-discovery."

—high school senior

"Whether you're a bold 'Tasman' who leads out loud or a steady 'Kepler' with quiet confidence, *Wisdom from the Wild for Youth* is the go-to guide for budding leaders—adolescents *and* adults alike. But this isn't just a book. It's a thoughtful, activity-packed road map for anyone looking to grow their leadership muscles (without the boring lectures). Real teen voices? Check. Fun animal facts? Double check. Reflective prompts that don't feel like homework? Yep. Grab a copy for your kiddo (or sneak one for yourself) and let Julie, her amazing teens, and maybe even a basking shark, show you the way."

—Taylor Gilley, PhD, director, staff learning and development, Houston Zoo

"The authors have created an interactive and adventurous experience to inspire youth leaders. With real-world skills that will translate throughout adulthood, this book is perfect for any curious reader looking to learn about leadership in a way they'll never forget!"

—Reese Scholl, college sophomore, Liberty University

"Whether you are young in age or young in spirit, *Wisdom from the Wild for Youth* is an inspirational read that balances childhood curiosity with lifelong lessons. Julie, Tasman, and Kepler emphasize that growth is a journey and mistakes along the way are more than just okay–they're encouraged!"

—Greer Gaspard, college freshman, Florida Gulf Coast University

WISDOM FROM THE WILD

FOR YOUTH

JULIE C. HENRY

WITH *TASMAN HENRY & KEPLER HENRY*

WISDOM *FROM THE* WILD

LEADERSHIP TALES WITH *TAILS*

GREENLEAF
BOOK GROUP PRESS

Published by Greenleaf Book Group Press
Austin, Texas
www.gbgpress.com

Distributed by Greenleaf Book Group

For ordering information or special discounts for bulk purchases, please contact Greenleaf Book Group at PO Box 91869, Austin, TX 78709, 512.891.6100.

Design and composition by Greenleaf Book Group
Original chapter illustrations by Kevin Stone and Olivia Stone
Cover design by Greenleaf Book Group and Brian Phillips
Cover images used under license from Shutterstock.com; Istock.com

Publisher's Cataloging-in-Publication data is available.

Print ISBN: 979-8-88645-379-9

eBook ISBN: 979-8-88645-380-5

To offset the number of trees consumed in the printing of our books, Greenleaf donates a portion of the proceeds from each printing to the Arbor Day Foundation. Greenleaf Book Group has replaced over 50,000 trees since 2007.

Printed in the United States of America on acid-free paper

25 26 27 28 29 30 31 32 10 9 8 7 6 5 4 3 2 1

First Edition

FROM JULIE

For Dr. Ann, Dr. Kaufman, Mr. Uhl, and Penny—who encouraged this young leader to choose her own adventure

FROM TASMAN

For Mrs. Poz's 2nd graders—who are leaders already

FROM KEPLER

For Mom
(Dad—you get the next book)

CONTENTS

"Your tendency to be inward-directed or outward-directed is huge; it governs every part of the way you live and work and love."

—Susan Cain, author of *Quiet: The Power of Introverts in a World That Can't Stop Talking*

. . .

"There is a time for stillness, but who hasn't also wanted to scream with delight at being outdoors? To simply announce themselves and say, I'm here, I exist?"

—Aimee Nezhukumatathil, author of *World of Wonders: In Praise of Fireflies, Whale Sharks, and Other Astonishments*

. . .

"I know how it looks. But just start. Nothing is insurmountable."

—Lin-Manuel Miranda, Pulitzer Prize–, Grammy-, Emmy-, and Tony Award–winning songwriter, actor, producer, and director; creator of Broadway's *Hamilton*

. . .

"They always say that time changes things, but you actually have to change them yourself."

—Andy Warhol, artist, leading figure in the Pop Art movement

HEY, READER!
YOU ARE A LEADER NOW

Yes, you read that right. You are a leader.

Yes, *you*. Right *now*.

Period.

Not tomorrow, not when you are older, not when you are chosen as captain for the team, not when you are selected as first chair in band, not when you have a college degree, not after you get better grades, not when you get your first (or next) job or even a different job title (or description) that has the word "leader" in it.

Today.

And if you already are the captain? The first chair in band? Finished your college degree and are proud of your grades? Working at a job you love and have a title that includes leadership responsibilities? Fantastic—that's even more of a reason to lean in a little closer and critically reflect on how you can continue growing as a leader.

I'm excited to share six Leadership Tales with you—a mash-up of leadership lessons + animal insights + simple steps to help you unleash the leader within—because I truly believe this combination can spark your interest and help you grow. Although not all of the animals in these Tales have *actual* tails (some are even plants—ha!), we call them "Leadership

Tales with Tails" because each lesson will come with a wildlife guide. But I don't want you to rely solely on my adult perspective; my teenagers, Tasman and Kepler, will be sharing their experiences and wisdom in this book too—not just because they are closer in age to you but also because they are vastly different people and lead in vastly different ways.

Honestly, if we had our way, we'd prefer to meet you in person and head out into nature together to learn leadership lessons directly from the source. Rather than sit together behind a desk or watch a presentation about leadership principles, we could put on metaphorical glasses with leadership lenses to observe and reflect on the animals and plants around us. How are they unique? How are they designed to survive in the wild? What insights can we glean from them about leadership?

Why? Because leadership is not a list of bullet points, step-by-step directions, or even a cookie-cutter plan to follow each time. Leadership is a critical thinking skill; it's a choose-your-own adventure activity. Maybe you hold a formal leadership position (like being the captain or point person on a project), so you are expected to make the decisions. Or maybe no one in your group of friends can decide where to go to dinner or which movie to watch, so you become the informal leader and offer a suggestion, listen to the opinions, and then make the final call—this is leadership too. Whether you are formally or informally the leader, the scenario you find yourself in will be different the next time; I guarantee it.

This is why Tasman, Kepler, and I would prefer to take you outside with us to think critically about leadership. Every time we go outside, we experience familiar things: The trees look the same as yesterday, we recognize the birds that live in our backyard, and we know the lizards that cruise along the pathways outside our home (at least they do where we live in Florida!). But then, we begin to notice things that are different or even unfamiliar: Why is there a hole underneath this tree now? Who dug this hole? What is it for? Is there an animal inside the hole? Should we reach our hand down the hole to find out? (That last question came directly from Kepler, and yes, he always wants to reach his hand into the unknown to discover more.)

As a leader—whether this is a title you have or a role you've assumed in the moment—you may have a plan. You might already know how you want to lead a discussion, divvy up responsibilities, and motivate people to action. But just like seeing unfamiliar things in nature, sometimes things do not go according to plan. In fact, *many* times, they don't go according to plan!

That's why, from the very beginning of this book, we want you to lean away from planning and lean into preparation. We will share leadership lessons and challenge you to act, not so that you have a *plan* for leadership but so that you are *prepared* as a leader. Then, when things inevitably surprise you or threaten to throw you off your game, you can feel secure knowing you are prepared for this moment, even if things are not going according to your original plan. Just like wanting to stick your hand down a hole outdoors to discover if an animal is living there, you'll be prepared for the often-unexpected result.

Tasman, Kepler, and I realized that although we can't take you all outdoors with us, we can do the next best thing: We've brought the outdoors to you by infusing insights from wildlife and wild places throughout this book to make leadership principles more understandable, memorable, and fun. Leadership can be as hard as it is exciting, so let's spend some time laughing about ladybugs and cacti as we learn leadership skills! Nature also helps level the leadership playing field. It doesn't matter how long you've held a leadership position, how much time you've spent studying leadership, or even the number of years you've lived on the Earth; nature can always be a common ground to have conversations about leadership principles. Your journey as a youth leader may be both exciting and nerve-racking. This book is intended to meet you where you are, recognizing and appreciating your experience and expertise as a leader today—and, of course, the unique leader that you are.

Many of you might see yourself in my daughter, Tasman, who leads "out loud": Tasman is eighteen years old, a freshman in college, and has been an avid communicator since before she could speak. She will jump right in to talk to you, learn more about you, challenge you, and champion you.

Tasman has never had stage fright. She will advocate for others as strongly as she will advocate for herself. She is just as comfortable in a group of people as she is by herself. She needs to balance highly engaged activities with downtime listening to music and reading (preferably outdoors by the ocean).

Perhaps you're more like my sixteen-year-old son, Kepler, and would rather keep to yourself. Kepler is a junior in high school, and his whole life, he has been a quiet, confident, go-with-the-flow type of person. He wants to explore at his own pace and be creative as often as possible. He is kind to everyone he meets. Kepler is not concerned with who or what is popular, what's trending on social media, or what's being discussed at lunch. He knows who he is, lets others be who they are, prefers a small number of deep friendships, and is fiercely loyal. He is an adrenaline seeker when he wants to be and an observer of life at other times.

For all of you who flex between high-octane energy and craving alone time and space, I, too, began life as a quiet, introspective person who much preferred letting others take the lead—until I discovered what I was passionate about. I realized that I loved to sing, that I couldn't wait until the next science class, and that I was fascinated by photography. Ever since I learned that I could leverage my time speaking at a microphone into making people laugh, learn, and even shed a tear, I haven't been able to stop dreaming and doing. Today, my leadership style is built on enthusiasm and energy, getting to know people, pushing for big ideas, and never being satisfied with the status quo—along with a healthy dose of trekking alone outdoors.

So, readers (who are also leaders), throughout your whole life, you will keep learning new skills. Many of these will be technical, how-to-do-something-concrete skills, like changing a tire or painting a picture. You'll get a new project in school and need to understand the expectations and how you will be graded. You'll try a new sport and need to learn the rules and how to play the game. You'll need to know how to operate a specific computer program or enter numbers into a spreadsheet. You'll practice communicating in various languages or follow performers on a stage with high-powered lighting systems. You'll rehearse interview skills, purposefully choose how to present yourself professionally, and commit yourself to continuing education no matter what job or career you select.

What do all of these options have in common? They involve people. Your classmates are people. Your teammates are people. Your teachers and professors are people. Your customers are people. Your supervisors are people. Your employees are people. Your network is composed of . . . ? People.

And when you are the leader—of a project, of a team, of a club, at school, at work, in the community, or anywhere else—you need to know *how* to lead, which means how to work with people. Sometimes you are chosen as the leader because of your experience, years of dedication, or many other reasons. But do not equate "how to do the technical bit" with "how to lead people"; these are distinctly different skills. They can be complementary, and it certainly helps to know the technical piece, but sometimes, leadership skills are described as *soft* skills. I encourage you to elevate your understanding and appreciation of these skills so that they move from *soft* to *essential*—because if you don't understand how to lead, it doesn't matter how well you know how to play the game; your teammates may not actually follow you onto the field.

BOTTOM LINE #1? Leadership is a *skill*. It can be taught, grown, and refined. It is a skill you will need throughout your life—whether you lead a country or just yourself. And the world needs you to show up as the leader you already are so you can leverage your unique perspective for maximum impact.

BOTTOM LINE #2? How you lead is unique to *you*. This is true no matter how you define your personality—introvert, extrovert, or anything in between; no matter what activities you're involved with, classes you like in school, or role models you have in your life; no matter if people tell you often how amazing your leadership skills are or if you never hear these comments from teachers, coaches, or others.

BOTTOM LINE #3? The time to start (or continue) growing your leadership skills is *now*. There are projects to start, people to motivate, and innovations to champion that are just waiting for you and your unique (essential!) leadership skills.

This is why infusing your leadership development with lessons from nature is so key to your leadership development journey: Every animal, plant, fungus, and bacterium is unique and has a place, and they are all essential. Some are sought after and praised for how amazing they are, and some you've never even heard of (even though they play an important role in their ecosystem). Think lions are the best or the only leaders in the animal kingdom? Elephants? Eagles? Dolphins? All due respect to these creatures, we've got a lot more wildlife wisdom in store for you beyond the typical "charismatic megafauna of leadership."

You belong—just as you are.

You wouldn't argue with a giant squid, would you?

IN CASE YOU WERE WONDERING . . .

Kepler: The way I see the world is drastically different from the world my mom and my sister see. They see the world in science terms while I see everything like a comic book. For example, if a ball gets thrown, I still calculate where it's going to land, but I see all the effects and noises. So, the cover and interior pages of our book are designed with a comic book look and feel because we thought it would be a fun way to balance the scientific information and because of the way I (and maybe you?) see the world.

HEY, READER! IT'S TASMAN

Leaders can come from all parts of the room, but I'm the type of leader who feels comfortable at the podium. I feel safe on a stage and find comfort when my voice is being heard. Maybe that sounds like you too.

I've been told I'm a leader in every aspect of my life because of my extremely outgoing nature. I've also been told to "tone it down" just as frequently. Perhaps you've been told that too. This book is an opportunity for all of us (including me) to learn (or be reminded) that "too much" is a myth. My leadership is loud. I am a lion who roars. And just like me, you are a leader who is not only allowed but who also should be celebrated. You are a leader today.

HEY, READER! IT'S KEPLER

Talking to people isn't really my thing, but I'm told you don't have to talk to people that much to be a leader. I like to call myself a lazy ambitious person, but I'm not *actually* lazy. I just need to find something I *really* enjoy doing to start driving toward it. But once I find that something and like doing it, I can become very successful at whatever that is.

FROM US AS YOUTH TO YOU

A LADYBUG AND A ROBOT

Throughout the book, Tasman and Kepler will ground in truth the principles I'm teaching you and share their experiences with wildlife and wild places. In short, they help me keep it real. They tell it like it is, from their views of the world, unfiltered and as honestly as possible. As we've all explained, they are independent thinkers with their own unique perspectives. But instead of asking you to take my (or their) word for it, the best thing I can do is share our favorite story that succinctly illustrates who they are as people and as leaders.

When you walk into our house, the first thing you come face-to-face with is a bright red wall with giant multicolored painted letters that spell out "the Kids Fort." The fort is actually a closet that we never used, but one day, I got frustrated by the boring closet doors greeting everyone who came to our home. In an unusual burst of creative home-decorating inspiration, I pulled up a YouTube video on how to remove closet doors, kept at it until the doors somehow came off, and then handed my two children (ages eleven and twelve at the time) some random jars of paint, a couple of brushes, and an assortment of stencils. They looked at me, eyebrows raised, until I pointed to the empty closet. "Go for it," I said. And the Kids Fort was born.

Today, the entrance to our home is much more fun and invites people into our world. I don't know what people notice first, but for me, the best part of walking through the front door is being greeted by the best craft my kids have ever made. In the middle of the brightly painted red wall is a frame containing pieces of black, red, white, and pink craft foam along with googly eyes that were pieced together to create two ladybugs.

The two ladybugs are not my favorite because they're the most intricate, took the longest, or were the most creative; they're my favorite because they are the clearest reflection of who Tasman and Kepler are as people . . . and as leaders. In fact, if you look closely at the drawing at the beginning of the chapter, you may be wondering why I'm even talking about two ladybugs because only one is obviously a ladybug; the other is something else entirely.

The behind-the-scenes true story of this craft was that when Tasman and Kepler were ages eight and six, we went to an event at the local children's museum. Because it was the children's museum, it was a safe space for kids, so I didn't worry so much about where they were at all times. So it was not unusual for them to disappear for a few minutes at a time and then come running up to me to proudly show me what they'd just made or tell me about their latest adventure.

The day my kids presented these two ladybugs, I distinctly remember turning around, seeing their smiling faces, and accepting these foam-and-googly-eye creations as I said in my overly loud, super-supportive mom voice, "Wow! How awesome! I'm so proud of you! These are amazing!"

Then, I looked more closely at what I was holding and added, "So . . . what were you *supposed* to make?"

Both of them nodded enthusiastically and shouted, "LADYBUGS!"

To which I replied, "Oh! Awesome. Fantastic. Excellent." Pause. "But . . ."

Tasman jumped in: "I *know*! Look at *my* ladybug. All the legs are evenly spaced out. When I added hearts to the spots on her back, I made sure to alternate the colors so they were evenly distributed. *And* I wrote my name so everyone would know it's mine."

Then I looked at Kepler, who shrugged and mumbled nonchalantly, "Yeah, Mom, I know. I was *supposed* to make a ladybug. But I just *had* to make a robot."

This is who they are as people. One will always follow the rules, crave order, read the directions multiple times, jump in first to explain, and make lists to check off accomplishments.

And one will always make robots.

When I encourage and challenge you to lead in the way you were born to lead, this is why: You are wired to learn, process, and see the world in a certain way, and this informs everything you do—including how you lead. My children see the world in two completely different ways, as was so clearly shown at the children's museum so many years ago.

I do not want to change who Tasman and Kepler are, especially because we need all kinds of perspectives as leaders. But I also cannot change them. I literally had no idea where they were in the museum, but off they went together, to the same classroom, with the same instructor, with the same materials, with the same directions, to make the same craft.

And they proudly brought me a ladybug and a robot.

Kepler: I've always liked this story because it shows my need to like something to get it done. When everyone else is making ladybugs, I'm glad to be the one kid with a robot. If you made a robot when everyone else made ladybugs, you might not be proud of it. But you *should* be proud because that means you saw an angle that nobody else saw. A good team isn't made up of people who all have the same skillset; what makes a good team is having many different skillsets and ideas to get the job done.

Tasman: Ten years later, I am still proud of this craft. I love that even as a kid, I felt compelled to go above and beyond my beloved instruction set. To me, it's not about having the *best* ladybug; it's about creating something *to the best of your ability*. That means always being equally proud of the kids who might have the creativity to make robots yet choosing to make your own beautiful, orderly ladybug instead.

READY, LEADER? LET'S DIVE IN AND SEARCH FOR GIANT SQUID

"With its untold depths, couldn't the sea keep alive such huge specimens of life from another age, this sea that never changes while land masses undergo almost continuous alteration? Couldn't the heart of the ocean hide the last-remaining varieties of these titanic species, for whom years are centuries and centuries millennia?"

—**JULES VERNE,** *TWENTY THOUSAND LEAGUES UNDER THE SEA*

Over the side of the boat and here we go!

Wait. Maybe we should know a few things first, like where in the world is this boat? How cold is the water? Are the seas rough or calm? How deep are we planning on diving? For how long? Is it daytime or nighttime? Who are we diving with? What kind of gear did we bring? And how long ago did we do our training, and do we remember anything??

And since you mentioned giant squid . . . is there a map or field guide that points in the direction of where to find them? No? We just jump in and search? What do we do with all of our time until then? What if we encounter something and we don't know what it is? What if something goes wrong underwater? What if half of our group wants to swim in one direction and the other half wants to stay where we are to observe an animal? How do we even communicate underwater? And why, if I have so many questions, are we just moving along and diving in before I have all the answers?

What do you mean I have to trust my training and lean into feeling uncomfortable? Did you just say that you have confidence that I am well prepared to figure it out on my own?

Hold up; this is supposed to be a book about leadership. Yet we're talking about giant squid . . . ? You probably picked up this book because you would like to know more about how to lead. And that's exactly what we get to in our Tales: teaching you concepts and action steps so you know more about *how* to lead.

Being a leader is like rolling over the side of a boat into the sea. You take all of what you've learned and prepared for with you as you face head-on the realities of each situation and each person you are leading. As the leader, you'll find that the possibilities are as vast as you can imagine and the unknowns as deep as the sea. Your training is crucial in preparing you to develop the trust you must have in your skillset for the rest of the journey. Underwater, like in leadership, fear can live next to awe, and exhaustion can fuel innovation. Every situation will both encourage and challenge you to know how to lead.

I want you to think about this book as a training manual for leadership—one that will prepare you just enough to make your own decisions. Notice that I have not yet said that this book will teach you what to do as a leader in every situation. Don't get me wrong; there are action steps in every chapter and concrete takeaways. But the overarching tenet of this book is *how* rather than *what*. That way, when you are faced with an opportunity or a situation that you may not have read about before, you can channel the preparation we've talked about so you know *how* even if you don't know exactly *what* to do yet. You will know because you will trust your training and lean on your gut instinct, which will be grounded in the six Leadership Tales to come.

Excited yet? Me too. And I am 100% confident that this type of preparation and training is what you need as a leader because—in addition to my own experience as a leader and in training leaders—this is how I was trained as a scuba diver. I was taught and then practiced skillsets that I needed as I explored underwater.

If you are brand new to learning about and practicing skills as a leader, you are like a person just beginning scuba dive training. For you, reading this book will be like the three to four days of classroom learning followed by putting the skills into action in a pool before getting into an open body of water, such as a lake or the ocean. It's an intensive process, as it should be: You are literally carrying your life-support system on your back, so you need to know how to make decisions when things are going right—or wrong.

After all that hard work, you will be certified as an Open Water Diver. Hooray! So this means you get to explore anywhere you want to in the ocean, right? Not exactly. You are now qualified to head underwater to a depth of . . . 60 feet (18 meters).

For those of you who have been in leadership positions at school, at a job, on a team, in a club, etc., reading this book might be like training to become an advanced scuba diver. You've mastered the basic skills, have some experience, and are now ready to learn and grow more. You want to dig into more advanced concepts, apply them to new scenarios, and expand your mind about possibilities. If you were training to become an Advanced Open Water Diver, you would build on your foundational skills and learn more on a deep dive, an underwater navigation dive, and three other dives. Then, congratulations! You are advanced certified. You are now qualified to head out and explore down to a depth of . . . 100 feet (30 meters).

Both of these certifications—and no matter whether you consider yourself a beginning or more advanced leader—are rigorous and lead to amazing opportunities. But let's put them into context:

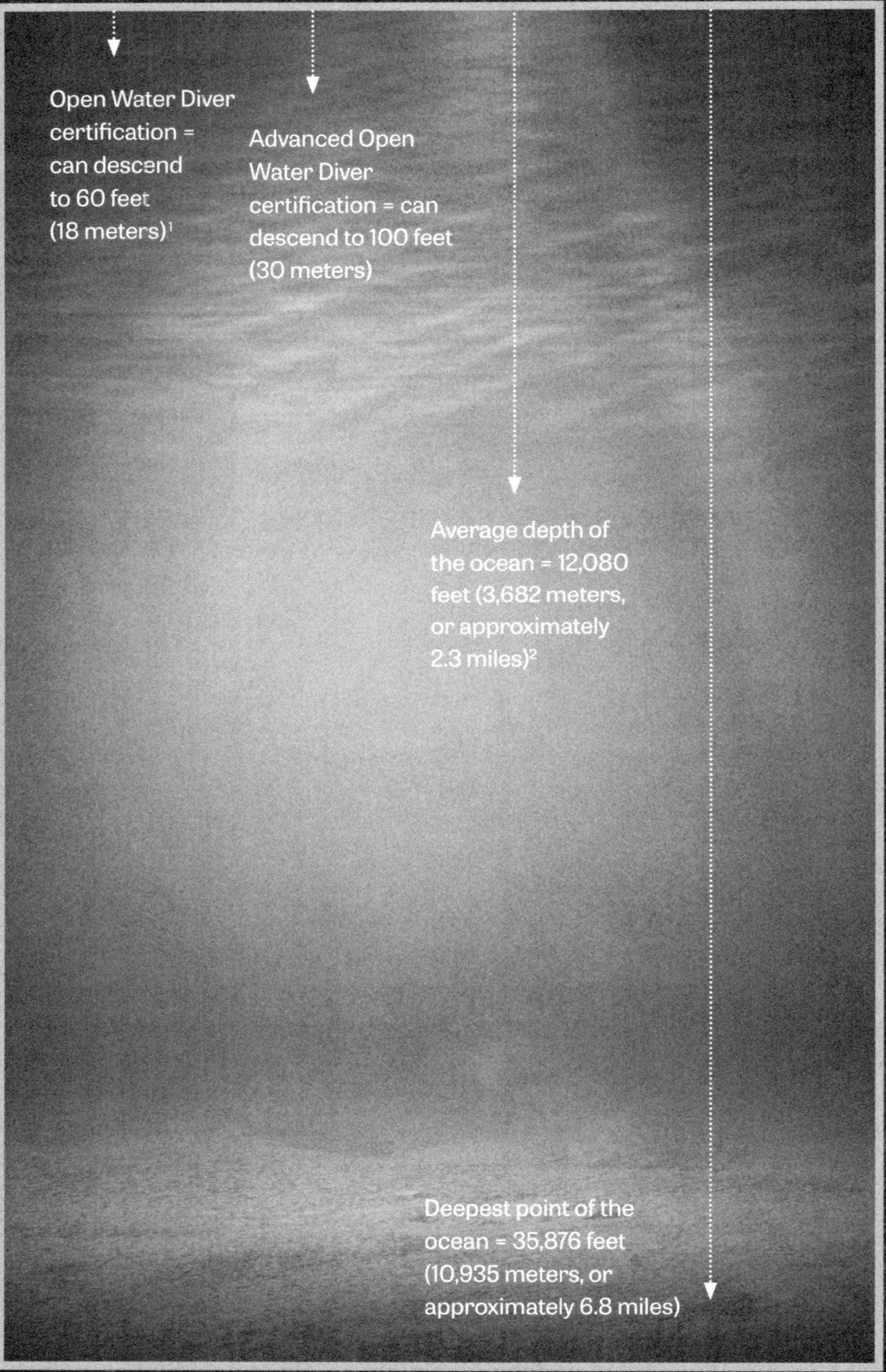

Open Water Diver certification = can descend to 60 feet (18 meters)[1]

Advanced Open Water Diver certification = can descend to 100 feet (30 meters)

Average depth of the ocean = 12,080 feet (3,682 meters, or approximately 2.3 miles)[2]

Deepest point of the ocean = 35,876 feet (10,935 meters, or approximately 6.8 miles)

DIAGRAM 1: DEPTH OF THE OCEAN COMPARED TO HOW DEEP A DIVER CAN GO

As you hold this book in your hands, do you feel excited about everything you can accomplish as a leader? Nervous that you will encounter an unknown situation? Ready to tackle anything that you face? Wary of what's yet to come?

All of these things are true, and you will feel these things throughout your journey as a leader. Why? The ocean is almost 7 miles at its deepest point. A trained scuba diver can explore roughly 0.17% of that depth, and an advanced diver can explore roughly 0.28%. Every book you read, podcast you listen to, mentor you learn from, and course that you take will continue to help you grow as a leader. But from the beginning, I want you to recognize that there is no actual way you can learn everything there is to know about how to lead and what to do in every single scenario because leadership is as vast as the ocean. I know that this can make you either nervous or excited or somewhere in between. But since it's a fact and you can't change this reality, you can adopt a mindset that helps you prepare and approach your leadership ocean.

Let me give you a real-life leadership example that you've most likely experienced: Have you ever been driving down the road with your friends singing loudly along to music in the car, and suddenly, you need to make a decision about what to do to keep everyone safe? Maybe the car in front of you blows a tire, so you need to swerve out of the way, but you need to be careful of the cyclists in the bike lane, and you're well aware that someone is following too closely behind you as you are coming up to a red light, all while being slightly distracted by the blaring music and your friends singing at the top of their lungs. So what do you do? Which decision do you make first?

Did you read about this exact scenario in one of the books in driver's ed or practice this before you got your license? Or is this an entirely new scenario but still related to the driver's ed training you've received? More than likely, all of these factors you may have learned separately in driver's ed and practiced theoretically in the car before, but maybe they've never all come together in the moment. So suddenly, here it is—the decision that technically you've never made before, but you can feel instinctively what you need to do and how you need to do it. So you ask your friends to be quiet, turn down the music, place both hands on the wheel, and keep everyone safe. Even if your friends may not have been paying attention in the moment and get upset when you turn down the music, they'll be happy you made that decision. Excellent job, leader.

Here's a practical example from my time as a leader: I was leading a team of people, and we were very excited that a project we were working on was about to come to an end. We had poured our blood, sweat, and tears into the last few months. Then, I received an email from my boss informing me about a last-minute change of direction. This was a decision totally out of my hands and one I could not push back on. And truthfully? I was more than a little upset; I was downright mad and could only see problems ahead.

The first problem was that I fundamentally disagreed with the decision. The next problem was that my team was now frustrated—and very vocal about it. The third problem was that I was stuck in the middle: I disagreed with this new decision, but it was my responsibility to keep the project moving forward. Yet my team was so upset about it that I had to figure out how to communicate to them the new direction, motivate them to take action, and not exactly hide my feelings (because they would be able to see I was doing that). At the same time, I could not disrespect my leaders who had made the new decision. I had received plenty of training on how to motivate teams, how to deal with conflict, how to keep projects moving, and how to manage change overall. But all of my training and all of my application of skills were not exactly helpful in the moment. I did not know what to do.

So, since I didn't know *what* to do, I decided to think differently and figure out *how* to lead instead: How could I keep the team from falling apart, rally us around a direction we did not want to take, keep my boss happy, and move the project forward yet stay true to myself as a leader? I made the best decision I could, worked through the inevitable angst and anger of the members of my team, channeled my personal frustration, and got us across the finish line. Whew. I was exhausted.

Each of these examples required you and me to trust that we were prepared to make the best decisions we could in the moment. We had to think about *how* to lead first and then decide *what* to do. Whether we knew it or not, we were actively embracing the fact that leadership is a critical-thinking skill. And it may not follow the steps you've learned in exactly the same order or even resemble what you've learned at all because real-time leadership is just that: happening in *real time*.

Getting ready to jump off the side of the boat together into our leadership ocean requires deep trust in each other. In honor of this mutual trust, here are our three promises to you:

1. **Acknowledgment and Acceptance:** This is a welcoming and inclusive space where we agree to acknowledge and accept where we are on our leadership journeys. No "I should have already" or "Why didn't I think of that before?"—all "We're glad you're here" and, most importantly, "We've got you!"
2. **Safe but Not Comfortable:** We promise to share ideas and challenge you in a way that makes you feel safe enough to consider what you didn't yet know or haven't tried—but not comfortable, because that's where the growth happens!
3. **More of the Leader That You Already Are:** Ultimately, we want you to grow even more into the way you naturally lead; there is a unique lens through which you see the world—and lead—and this is what you can lean more into now.

So let's go—over the side of the boat together, fully trained and prepared, remembering that 95% of the ocean is unexplored.[3] There are no roadways, traffic signals, or directional cues. There is open water in every direction, and we get to choose our own adventure.

Just like leadership.

And remember that giant squid we might encounter?

Scientists only knew they even existed because we would find their bodies in the bellies of sperm whales,[4] floating at the surface, or even trapped in large deep-sea fishing nets. There's a potentially 66-foot-long animal[5] swimming around in the ocean directly—but usually very deep—below where we play, fish, and dive, and we'd never seen it alive in its natural habitat for centuries (unless it came up to the surface when it was dying or already dead) until scientists innovated ways to record it on film in the deep sea.[6] There was no field guide for how to find a giant squid alive; scientists had to create one.

Your leadership ocean is directly in front of you. The Leadership Tales with Tails that follow are stories from nature with leadership principles. And while there are six in this book, we hope you are inspired to think of a few on your own too.

Then, what comes next? As you dive into your leadership ocean, how will you discover your own giant squid? That remains to be seen.

But what I do know? Each of you will do it in *your own way*.

LEADERSHIP FIELD GUIDE: HOW IT STARTED

"Even the greatest was once a beginner.
Don't be afraid to take that first step."

—Muhammad Ali, PROFESSIONAL BOXER AND ACTIVIST

If you want to measure growth and chart progress, you must begin with a benchmark or assessment to see where you started. This is what your teacher is doing when they give you a test on the first day of class; you might feel stressed because you don't know any of the answers, but this helps them figure out how to structure the course and teach you what you need to learn. Or if you want to become a faster runner in cross-country, you might first do a mile time trial to see how fast you currently are.

This is the point where you can check in with your leadership journey before you read any further and get more ideas. This benchmark is just for you; it does not have to be shared with anyone. It is not intended to be judgmental (remember the Acknowledgment and Acceptance promise?), but it is intended to be quantifiable, or easy to measure, so that you can reflect on your growth as a leader at the end of the book too.

Both of these exercises are intended to be relatively quick, and you will not reflect on them . . . yet. Beware the tendency to overthink; just answer to the best of your ability in the moment!

LEADERSHIP FIELD GUIDE EXERCISE #1: WHO AM I AS A LEADER?

For each prompt, answer quickly off the top of your head, and enter only one word per line. You don't have to fill up each line, but don't add more words than there are lines. At the end of this exercise, you will have between one and three words as answers to each prompt.

TODAY'S DATE: ________________

1. My best (or close) friend would say that as a leader, I am:

   ____

   ____

   ____

2. My favorite teacher would say that as a leader, I am:

   ____

   ____

   ____

3. My parent/guardian would say that as a leader, I am:

   ____

   ____

   ____

4. My classmates/teammates would say that as a leader, I am:

____

____

____

5. As a leader, I am:

____

____

____

LEADERSHIP FIELD GUIDE EXERCISE #2: WHAT DO I THINK LEADERSHIP IS ALL ABOUT?

In the box, first draw a picture of a leader doing leadership. I know that may seem ambiguous or too open-ended, but that is the point—off the top of your head, when someone says the word "leader" or you envision what leadership is all about, what do you see in your head? In the next five (no more) minutes, draw it on the next page. After completing your drawing, answer the question at the bottom.

After completing both of these exercises, don't make any changes, edits, or judgments. The date you wrote down will help you when you get to the field guide at the end of the book and reflect to see just how much you've thought about leadership and intentionally decided who *you* want to be as a leader.

Now, turn the page. Six Tales with Tails about leadership are just waiting to be discovered.

TODAY'S DATE: ______________

Draw a picture of a leader doing leadership.

What is happening in your picture?

____

____

____

____

LEADERSHIP TALE #1

"GREAT" LEADERSHIP IS A MYTH . . . THE REALITY IS SO MUCH BETTER

(THINK DRACULA WAS THE ULTIMATE FANGED LEGEND? LET'S ASK THE VAMPIRE BATS)

"There was a full moonlight, and I could see that the noise was made by a great bat, which wheeled round—doubtless attracted by the light, although so dim—and every now and again struck the window with its wings."

—*BRAM STOKER,* DRACULA

I love the time of night as the sun is setting, the weather is cooling down, the sounds start changing, and the birds fluttering around suddenly start to look just a bit different . . . because they're not birds at all; they're bats!

Where I live, the bats love the time right at dusk, and we love to sit outside and watch them swoop energetically around in circles consuming any number of (what I imagine to be) delicious bugs. So, of course, any time I'm at a zoo with a nocturnal house (which houses animals that are most active at night and sleep all day) or an exhibit that might include bats, I immediately head that way. I walk purposefully past expansive habitats with tigers, bears, giraffes, and even African painted dogs where most people are standing and watching animal behavior.

Instead, I'm on a quest for my favorite free-flying exhibit, where you walk along a dimly lit pathway and the bats can swoop all around you. Usually, the species of bats are so large, I can easily notice them coming toward me, but every now and then, a much smaller species of bat suddenly appears next to my ear. I'm instantly aware that it must have come zooming up from behind, appearing before I even knew it was there, and I am reminded just how silently they can fly.

And, of course, there are some of my favorite behind-the-scenes moments at the zoo, such as when I've been prepping for an overnight sleepover program alongside zookeepers who are getting food ready for the bats. As I unload boxes of cookies, bags of chips, and cartons of juice boxes, the keepers are setting out small dishes and pouring from a large bottle of red liquid—scrumptious blood that the vampire bats will soon be feasting on.[1]

Bats have incredibly innovative adaptations, at least from a human's point of view, such as echolocation (producing sounds to help them navigate in the dark) and giving birth while hanging upside down.[2] It's no wonder they have inspired countless myths and legends like that of Dracula.

But to me, the real animal is always more fascinating than any imagined story (kind of like the saying "the truth is always stranger than fiction"). And so off to the bat exhibit I trek, hoping for yet another glimpse of a bat hanging by its feet, slowly unfolding from its tightly curled position. I am instantly captivated as the bat unfurls each wing, revealing slightly transparent skin covering prominent bumps and five elongated structures in a very familiar pattern—bones that mimic the pattern of a human hand and arm. Without consciously thinking about it, I instinctively extend my arm and uncurl my fingers, wondering what it would be like if I were uncurling my own bat wing instead.

CALLING ALL MYTH BUSTERS!

How many of you want to be a "great" leader?

Have you met what you consider great leaders? Maybe been on a team with one? Gotten a chance to work for or alongside one? Perhaps one of your teachers or professors showed great leadership skills? Or have you really admired how a classmate of yours handled a tricky scenario recently that required great leadership decisions?

Think about these questions for a minute. Are names or faces coming to mind? Maybe you can even conjure a few more examples of great leaders on your own.

Fantastic. Hold on to those names and faces in your head.

You must be thinking of *exactly* the same type of leader, and therefore the same type of person, for each answer. Right? And I'm sure your answers are the same as mine, Kepler's, and Tasman's, as well as those of the person sitting next to you and the one across the . . . after all, if we're going to talk about great leadership—and the only qualification is the word "great"—then all of these people must lead in the same way, right? And you need to lead the same way that they do because you want to become a great leader too.

No? Ah, that's because some of the people you are thinking about lead differently than the others. Or wait—do they *all* lead differently from each other? But I thought we were talking about great leaders overall?

This is similar to when I say the word "bat," and some of you might think about giant fruit bats while others might envision small brown bats. Some of you might think about flying foxes, and some immediately remember the character of Dracula or the movie *Hotel Transylvania*. Since there are more than 1,400 species of bats, chances are good we are not all thinking of the exact same species.[3]

If Dracula is just a character in a fictional book, why would he come to mind when I say the word "bat" in reference to a real animal? Well, one of the inspirations for the character of Dracula was a real person who was a fifteenth-century warlord. And if that's true (and also slightly terrifying), is it also possible that the inspiration for Dracula turning into a bat was inspired by an actual animal?[4] Yes. And they're called (wait for it . . .) vampire bats.

Let's think about myths and their origins. In the fifteenth century, there was a Romanian prince named Vlad Țepeș who became notorious for the brutal way he treated his enemies, earning him the nickname Vlad the Impaler.[5] In the early 1800s, scientists began writing about bats, which had been named vampire bats after mythical creatures in European folklore who also drank blood.[6] In his 1897 novel, *Dracula*, Bram Stoker used these two facts to create a fictional story about a person who drank blood and could turn into a bat.[7]

Similarly, if you look throughout history, you can find leaders in all walks of life, in every century, all across the globe. But if we try to describe them collectively and make one narrative (story) about them all as being great—and therefore that "great" leadership is the goal? That is fiction; it is a myth.

Why is this important? Because if you are striving to be a great leader, you will never achieve it because there are as many diverse examples of what it means to be a great leader as there are people themselves.

So how can you learn to be a leader? You have to start by defining what being a great leader actually means. Put words down on paper so you know what to aim for, which attributes you want to highlight, and which habits you want to learn. Then, you'll have concrete ideas on which to focus your energy and by which you can measure your progress.

Your first nugget of wisdom from the wild? "Great" leadership is a myth.

But stay tuned. Just like with Dracula and vampire bats, the reality is so much better.

THE TRUTH BEHIND THE MYTH

Remember those names and faces you brainstormed in the last section? The ones that you consider to be great leaders—even if they're different from the people in my head or your friends' heads, or even if you're the only one who thinks they are great leaders?

It's time to put actual words down about what being a great leader means. The big, overarching question I want you to think about is, "What are the characteristics or skillsets that make them a great leader?" Next are eight prompts to help you generate words or phrases that describe the leaders on your list. Following each prompt are Tasman's and Kepler's answers from when they did this exercise, which might inspire you and help provide guidance as you go through each one.

1. How does/did this leader get to know me?

Kepler: They talk to me; they listen to my ideas.

Tasman: They asked me about my experiences to understand my background and how it related to my sport so they knew better how to coach me; they asked me about my story and told me no detail is too small; they treat me like an individual person who has a unique story; they are approachable and open, talk to us about everything, and share their stories, too, to relate to us.

2. How does/did this leader interact with others?

Kepler: They're kind and friendly and help others.

Tasman: They're respectful, and they see everyone as equals; they treat people as if everyone has different abilities but everyone has the same possibilities; they want to understand everyone; they're kind, conversational, and easygoing.

3. What strategies do/did they use to communicate good news?

Kepler: They're direct, which I appreciate.

Tasman: They're usually more excited than I am because they want to celebrate everyone's successes; they make sure I understand the value of the information first and that everything has weight to it.

4. How do/did they motivate me to action?

Kepler: They recognize that I'm self-motivated.

Tasman: They give me options, or they give me a correlation/causation so that I can understand what I'm doing and why I'm doing it; people respect this leader so much, so they listen when the leader motivates us; they do whatever they can to make things fun.

5. What are the tactics they use(d) to deliver feedback I might not like?

Kepler: They're direct; I like critical feedback, and I don't get upset about feedback as long as it's actual feedback, which means giving me advice on how to make it better; they can't just say, "That's not good" but rather "That's not good, so what if we try . . ."

Tasman: It's presented as everything is an opportunity for growth (e.g., instead of "Tasman, you are weak," they state it as, "Tasman, you are not strong enough for that yet"); everything is in perspective (e.g., "You are more than a test grade"); it's never a detriment to who we are as students.

6. How does/did this leader set the vision or goals, and do/did they want my ideas?

Kepler: They brainstorm the goals and the ideas with us collectively, and then they ultimately put our ideas together based on their experience; we can still change and suggest ideas throughout the process.

Tasman: They have a plan and communicate the plan, but if their performers aren't happy, they know that the trick won't be performed well, so they want our input; they give us the big picture about what we're doing and where we're going, but they're open when we need help and give us opportunities to get help in the way we best need or want it; they are always open to input even though it is ultimately going to be their decision.

7. If I wanted to share an idea that was unpopular, or if I felt like I was failing or making mistakes, how would this leader react?

Kepler: They would help me.

Tasman: I don't expect them to just go with what I say, but I'm not afraid of expressing my opinion; they would put everything in perspective and then give me the help I need; they tell me that asking for help is a skill, and they encourage me to advocate for the help I need.

8. How do/did I know what this leader values or stands for as a person?

Kepler: The more you're around a person, the more you get to know them; their actions and their words are consistent and authentic; even when I meet someone for the first time, I can get a feel for their sense of humor and what their views are; I can learn more information about people than they tell me (through their behaviors, their body language, how they talk to others, and all that stuff).

Tasman: Through how they treat me and others; through how they communicate with other leaders and students; through their actions as well as their words.

In all of the answers, notice that the word "great" did not appear a single time. Once Tasman and Kepler started thinking about it, they had a lot to say about each of the leaders they admire. They would begin with only a few words, and then more and more descriptions came to mind. When I finally read their completed answers, I could understand how the characteristics and skillsets they described could combine to make these people great leaders—even though I had no idea who Tasman and Kepler had been thinking about. And honestly, even if they had told me the names of the leaders they were picturing in their heads, I would not have come up with the same words because the leaders had led them directly, not me. These answers are authentic to their personal experiences.

In the same way, the more concrete and direct your answers are, the more you can accurately capture what being a great leader mean to *you*. Then, you will be able to clearly see a pathway forward to the leadership skills you most admire, the ones you already possess, and the ones you want to learn more about.

YOU ARE MORE VAMPIRE BAT THAN VAMPIRE

As part of the inspiration for mythological vampires, vampire bats have the characteristics that make a vampire great and unique, like being nocturnal, flying with stealth, and drinking blood from its prey. The rest of the 1,400+ bat species? They share some of these characteristics but not all. A golden-capped fruit bat, for example, is far happier searching for a yummy piece of fruit rather than a small mammal on which to feast.

So those leaders you envisioned at the beginning of these chapters? I'm so thankful you have had them in your life. They are the leaders that inspire you to think critically about the characteristics that make a leader great. The words and phrases you wrote down about them? I'm sure you share some of these characteristics with them but not all. While some of the leaders you admire might be larger-than-life personalities who motivate you with grandiose statements and excessive enthusiasm, you might be the leader who prefers direct, unemotional statements and delivers praise infrequently but nonetheless still motivates your team to greatness.

Being a great leader is possible for all of us; it just might look a little different. This means you never have to compare yourself to another great leader or be afraid that you're not like another leader, even if you deeply admire them, because *you're not.* And you're not supposed to be.

Celebrate the great leaders around you for the way they lead.

Then, extend those beautiful wings, let go of the branch you're hanging on to upside down by your feet, head out into the darkness even if you can't actually see where you're going yet, and lead in your very own vampire bat way.

Kepler: Connecting Dracula to leadership is intriguing, and it caught my attention because I have never heard of leadership connected to Dracula before. I think this is a good connection because people are intrigued by things they've never seen before.

Tasman: I think that being a great leader means being yourself. "Lead in the way you were born to lead" is a phrase my mother says often, and it perfectly captures being great. "Great" is a word that can be interpreted in many different ways. It's completely subjective. The leaders I admire are great because they are exactly who they are meant to be. My mom is a great leader because she is always herself, whether she is teaching a room of successful businesspeople or talking to my cats. "Great" really is a stupid word; it means absolutely nothing. Each of us must lead as we were wonderfully designed to lead. Every leader is unique; it would be pretty boring if we were all the same.

LEADERSHIP IN REAL LIFE

When I was in high school, we had physical textbooks, and the school wanted to make sure they did not get damaged. So the first day of school always involved bringing paper bags to school and cutting, taping, and shaping them to cover our textbooks. By the time I was a senior in high school, I was pretty confident in my abilities to cover my textbook—that is, until third period, when I sat per usual chatting with my friends and cutting, taping, and shaping our brown paper bags to our books, when suddenly my teacher came by, ripped the paper out of my hand, and instructed me in a loud, firm voice, "Start over!" My rule-following heart was crushed, my high school ego was embarrassed, and not only did I decide then and there that I was going to hate this class, but it was also clear I was not going to get along with the teacher.

Then, I watched as she employed the same firm tactics with others in the class. She wasn't swayed by how much someone thought they knew already about the subject or how many questions people volunteered to answer. She had a plan, she had high expectations, and she let everyone know what they were. So I went along with this and decided that holding on to anger was only going to frustrate me, not her, so I started paying attention. And then actually learning. Then actually excelling. And liking the class.

The A that I earned that year in AP Calculus is one of my proudest grades because I had to not only work for it but also figure out how to work with a teacher with exceptionally high expectations and little tolerance for people who thought they knew better. I was used to learning things relatively quickly. Turns out it's hard (at least for me) to know anything about calculus before you actually learn it.

Fourteen years later, I invited her to my bridal shower. Last year, I sent her a Christmas card, as I do every year. Mrs. Molls was a great teacher because she was fair, knowledgeable, and dedicated to our success—even if it meant relearning how to cut, fold, and tape a paper bag to cover my textbook first before I could open it and learn math.

LEADERSHIP FIELD NOTES

- When you hear yourself describe someone as a great leader, take it one step further and add a few words or phrases to describe what makes them great.
- Pick a few words or one phrase that you brainstormed about what makes a leader great, and start intentionally working toward this as a goal for yourself.
- Have a discussion with a friend about what great leadership is really all about. Ask them their opinions and experiences, share yours, and strive to gain a new perspective into great leadership that you may not have considered before.

INTO THE WILD FOR A BRAIN BREAK

WITH TASMAN

Leatherback sea turtles are absolutely humongous. Like, they can get to be as heavy as a small car.[8] But as babies, they can fit in the palm of your hand! Last summer, I got the chance to help release little leatherbacks at a United Nations protected conservation site in Panama. We took walks every night to see if there were any mamas laying eggs. Never saw one, but the moon and the stars were so bright it was all worth it. As soon as we finished our four-hour walk on the second night, we were all told to "come quick" to the hatchery. A nest of baby turtles had been born!

The little babies were placed in a wheelbarrow and brought out to the water, where they were given about a 10-foot stretch of sand to figure out how to use their flippers until the waves picked them up. Baby turtles follow the reflection of the moonlight to get where they are going, so my team quickly turned off all headlamps as soon as the wheelbarrow was uncovered. Coincidentally, one of my instructors was walking along the beach to see if any turtles had fallen out—with his headlamp on and shining bright. I was crouched down and couldn't see anything not illuminated by the stars, but I could feel the leatherbacks scurrying away from the ocean.

"Turn your light out," my friend yelled to the instructor. "They think you're the moon!" The beach became pitch black once the light was out, and all movement around me stopped. It took the turtles a moment to reconfigure themselves, but eventually we heard the movement of flippers against sand as they rushed toward the raging waves. Five minutes later, they were all gone. I don't think I'll ever forget the feeling of flippers against my shoes as the babies rushed toward the ocean, knowing that one day they would return to that beach in order to lay their own eggs. I'm so proud to say that I was even a small part of their circle of life.

LEADERSHIP TALE #2

LEADERS COME IN ALL SHAPES AND SIZES . . . BUT STILL HAVE A FEW THINGS IN COMMON

(500+ SPECIES OF SHARKS, YET ALL SHARE FIVE DEFINING TRAITS)

"The sea should be enjoyed, the animals in it. When you see a shark underwater, you should say, 'How lucky I am to see this animal in his environment!'"

—DR. EUGENIE CLARK, "THE SHARK LADY," FOUNDER OF MOTE MARINE LABORATORY AND AQUARIUM

If you've ever been to summer camp, you know how much fun it can be, especially if you're craving unknown exploration, want to try out new things you may not be able to learn in school, and love the organized chaos of camp that comes along with the blissful, fun days of summer. And for those adults who teach summer camp? I'd like to say we do it primarily to give back to younger generations or because we might need a summer job, but secretly, I think it's really because we like to be kids again too.

And summer camp at a renowned marine laboratory, where world-famous scientists can walk by at any moment, and an associated aquarium that showcases a rarely seen giant squid—one of only fifteen on exhibit in the United States? Now *that* is another level entirely. When I ran the education programs at that marine laboratory and aquarium, I had to be equal parts prepared for the known and also ready for everything to change at a moment's notice.

I never knew what was going to happen day-to-day. Like when a dolphin jumped out of the water right outside our classroom window, completely distracting all of our middle-school summer campers and, let's be honest, me too. Or when one of the marine scientists called to tell me they'd just received a shark from Greenland to photograph and study and invited me and my campers to stop what we were doing and head over to watch. *Yes! Real science! In action!* With a shark none of us had ever seen before. To me, the answer to an invitation like that is always 100% yes.

So the days, weeks, months, and summer camp seasons continued, and I loved every single hectic and calm moment. I adored the kids' muffled screams of delight that came through their snorkels as they observed a sea star for the first time, laughed along with (most of) them when a giant horseshoe crab walked out of the seagrass in front of our masks, and applauded their calm movements so as to not disturb the nurse shark we found lying on the ocean floor. Most of the parents told me they wished they could be a part of our education programs as well because it had been their dream to study marine biology. They were usually as excited as their kids!

Until my office phone rang one day.

On the other end of the line, a mother explained in a quick tumble of words that she was sending her thirteen-year-old son from New York City to stay with his grandparents in Florida so he could attend our summer camp. She said he was very excited, and she quickly outlined how confident she was in what she had read in our camp materials so far. She went on about how much valuable information her son would learn about the sea and was ecstatic for him to have a chance to explore a new part of the States.

I nodded along, half listening but smiling at the typical excitement parents had shared with me over the years. I was getting ready to deliver my standard reply that went something like, "Yes, we'll take good care of him, and we're looking forward to having him here at camp with us too!" when her voice suddenly increased in volume, and she hit me with a question I'd never gotten before in all my years running the summer camp: "So now I need an *ABSOLUTE* guarantee that my son will *MOST DEFINITELY NOT* be in the *OCEAN* with *SHARKS . . . EVER*."

I paused, completely shocked and unsure of what to say next. For a moment, I thought she was kidding, but it turns out, no, absolutely not, she was definitely serious.

She'd clearly read all about the camp. Our marine laboratory had literally been founded by a shark scientist, and it currently housed scientists who constituted the *only* Center for Shark Research designated by Congress in the nation. So all of the summer camp students would, in fact, be wading, field sampling, and snorkeling in the ocean—not a sea pen, not an area roped off, but the open ocean.

"Well, ma'am," I began. "I respect and acknowledge your fears about sharks. Many people feel that way because sharks tend to get a bad rap in the media, and there are many stereotypes about these animals. But let me assure you, our marine laboratory was founded by the legendary ichthyologist Dr. Eugenie Clark in 1955, so sharks are not only part of our origin story, but they are also an active part of our current research. So we absolutely want our summer camp students to explore and be a part of that."

"So," she said, her voice continuing to rise, "what you're telling me is that my *SON* will be in the *WATER* with *SHARKS*?!"

"Yes," I replied calmly.

"Well, what do you *PLAN TO DO* if a shark swims nearby? How can you *KEEP HIM* from getting *HURT*? And *WHY* is this a *PART* of your summer camp plan?" She was shouting even louder now, and I had to hold the phone away from my ear.

I took a deep breath and replied, "All I can tell you for sure, ma'am, is that we'll be in the ocean, which is where the sharks live. So we're visitors in their home. And I can assure you they'll see us long before we even know they're there."

Silence on the other end of the line. Then, she said, "That's it? That's your answer?"

I could practically hear her gritting her teeth.

"Yes," I said, then paused. "Well, I could also share with you that I haven't lost a kid to a shark yet, and I don't plan to anytime soon."

She didn't appreciate my attempt at humor.

Two months later, her thirteen-year-old son arrived at camp. He was as eager as I'd ever seen anyone to walk into our building. And when it came time for our first excursion into the ocean? The one where sharks roamed freely among the snorkelers who were visiting their home?

He led the way.

His enthusiasm far outweighed any fear he might have felt about being in the water with sharks. He was curious and engaged and wanted to know the truth behind the stereotypes. And when it came time to move on to the next activity?

He was the last one out of the water.

ARE YOU SURE THAT'S A SHARK?

Sharks.

As you read that word, I know some of you are thinking, *Yes! Let's go! I'd love to be diving with sharks* right now*! I can't wait to see them up close, watch them as they swim, be in awe of their size, power . . .*

No way. Not ever! others of you are thinking. *There is not a chance I want to be anywhere near sharks. They are terrifying. Haven't you seen the movie* Jaws*? I'm happy to be on dry land and far away.*

Maybe you are relatively indifferent, thinking, *Hmmmmm, sharks. I wouldn't go out of my way to see them, but if they swam by me, that would be fine too. They can do their thing, and I'll keep doing mine.*

Sharks have long fascinated people, and they inspire emotions from awe and amazement to fear.[1] Most of these strong reactions can be attributed to the idea of a stereotypical shark: a larger-than-you animal with a big, heavy, grayish-colored body; a seemingly menacing look; laser-focused black eyes; sharply angled fins; and rows and rows of jagged, pointy teeth.

Of course, these types of sharks *do* exist—that's how we created the stereotype for a shark in the first place! Just look up pictures of a great white shark or turn on the movie *Jaws*, and you'll see an animal that aligns closely with this stereotypical version of a shark. So when you think of the word "shark," your mind probably doesn't first go to a nurse shark or a zebra shark, which both spend most of their time settled on the ocean floor. And it's rare that people connect "shark" with the biggest fish in the sea, the whale shark, which grows up to 60 feet (18 meters) but is considered a gentle giant swimming slowly through the water, filtering out plankton for food.

But if you *really* want to smash the stereotype of a shark, let's think about the thresher shark, which relies on its enormous 9-foot- (3-meter-) long tail (about half the length of its body!) as a weapon to stun prey. Or the basking sharks—one of my favorites—which swim around with their mouths open, using the five bright white sections in their mouths containing gill rakers to help them catch plankton. Or the Bahamas sawshark with its long snout lined with teeth. Or even the megamouth shark that was only discovered in 1976 and is seen so rarely that barely anything is known about it . . .[2]

I could go on and on about all of the fascinating species of sharks but then we'd be here awhile because, in reality, there are more than 500 species of sharks![3]

That's *a lot* of sharks.

And the majority of them do not look anything like the cliché version in your head. Yet scientists still call these 500+ species collectively "sharks," so they must have *some* things in common, right? Right! For scientists to group them together in what is called a "taxonomic key," they must all share at least a few characteristics.

To start with, sharks are fish, but they are vastly different from a tuna, barracuda, or clownfish. So what traits group sharks together, and what differentiates them from the other fishes of the world?

All 500 species of sharks share five defining traits.

And just as there are at least 500 different types of leaders, all leaders share five defining characteristics.

LEAD LIKE A SHARK

Whether it's a carpet shark lying on the ocean floor or a megamouth swimming in the deep sea, all sharks have the following:

1. A skeleton made from cartilage
2. Five to seven pairs of gills
3. Rigid dorsal fins
4. No swim bladder for buoyancy
5. Skin covered with dermal denticles

There's a lot more about sharks we could go into here, but I want to use this analysis of shark diversity and similarities to pull you back into the mindset of leadership skills, just as we did by exploring bats and the myth of great leadership.

Just like there are hundreds of species of sharks that all share five things in common, there are also defining characteristics that all leaders share. Each of these characteristics can be interpreted or executed differently by different leaders, yet those same characteristics still exist in every leader. (For those of you who like concrete ideas and definable actions, this should feel grounding.)

While I will continue to encourage you to lead in your unique way and define "great" in the way you want to lead, there are still definitive traits that all leaders must employ to lead effectively. And what better way to help us remember these five traits of leadership than by taking a cue from a SHARK?

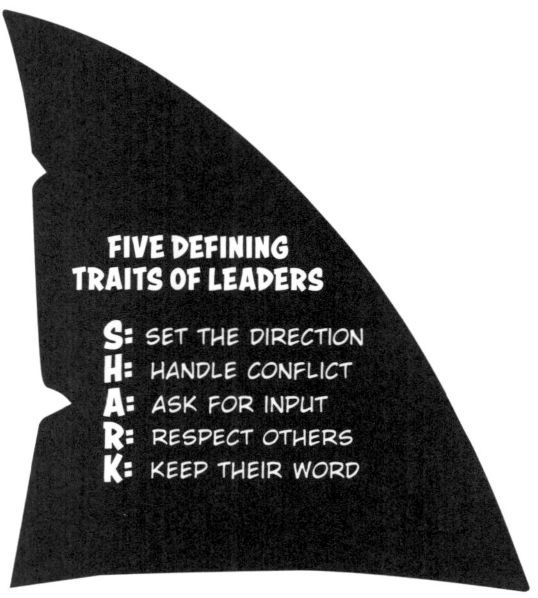

S: SET THE DIRECTION

Leaders always have the big picture in mind. They know the direction their group is heading, what they're trying to accomplish, and why they're doing it. Sometimes, this big picture might be called the vision or mission; at other times, the direction is toward specific goals and objectives. Regardless, the most important component is that you, as a leader, have a direction, so you don't feel like you're aimlessly lost and working for no reason.

For example, if you're leading the team in theater class that is working behind the scenes on the school's fall play, *The Lion, the Witch, and the Wardrobe*, you've ideally spent a lot of time thinking about the overall view of the production, such as what you want the play to look and feel like for everyone sitting in the audience. The atmosphere in the auditorium can influence what the set design will look like.

You'd also consider things like how to make the set look magical when the characters arrive in the land of Narnia. And how can you best show the audience the White Witch is *not* to be trusted—before she utters a single word? You'll think about how the sound system can add to the ambience and what your team should wear each night so that they add to rather than detract from the experience. Lucky for you, leader, one of the really fun parts about putting on a school play is creating this complete experience for the audience.

As a leader who sets the direction, you should remain deeply committed to the vision. You'll keep your team in the loop so they understand the big picture, but just enough so they don't get overwhelmed and can stay focused on their individual tasks. With so many team members, it is easy for there to be lots of different ideas about, for instance, what the wooden wardrobe that leads to the land of Narnia should look like, how the costumes will add to the storyline, or what kind of music could really up the suspense. But someone has to set the primary direction for the play . . . for the team.

Ultimately, you as the leader are responsible for making sure the team's work continues in a focused manner and learning how to make smart course adjustments as needed along the way toward your end goal—whether or not that involves creating a magical world of fauns, satyrs, dryads, centaurs, and a talking lion.

H: HANDLE CONFLICT

I don't know many people who enjoy conflict, myself included, so this one might not be your favorite, but it is absolutely a core characteristic that all leaders share. Whenever there are people working, playing, or interacting together, conflict is bound to arise, no matter how well a project is going or even if everyone is already friends.

Conflict doesn't mean there's a knockdown, drag-out fight or a loud war of words. Conflict can be any sort of disagreement or misunderstanding that could, if unchecked, lead to resentment or turmoil within the team. In short, beware the tendency to ignore conflict or try to just wait until it all blows over and everyone gets along again. Accept the fact that conflict will happen, and resolve that you, as the leader, will (and can) handle it.

When conflict inevitably does arise, it's not necessarily because you've done something wrong as the leader. The conflict might not be related to you at all. But it *is* your responsibility as the leader to address and help resolve the conflict. Ignoring the conflict will not make it go away; it will continue to fester and grow so when you eventually do address it, it will be that much harder to resolve.

For instance, if you are leading the five-person team responsible for bringing drinks and snacks for your homeroom's end-of-quarter celebration and three people don't bring their assigned food, other team members and classmates will be understandably frustrated (and thirsty or hungry!), which could lead to snide remarks, rude looks, resentment—overall conflict. You, as the leader, must step in to handle the conflict and help ease the situation, ideally before any tempers flare.

This example of the Great Snacker Slacker Scandal is pretty straightforward in terms of conflict resolution. You can talk to the team members directly to find out why they didn't follow through and bring the assigned snacks. You can nicely ask them to change their behavior the next time, explaining how it affected others on the team and in the class. Then, you can assure your other team members that you have handled the problem before they get even more mad with those people and take the situation into their own hands (perhaps literally—*food fight!*). Most importantly, at the end of the next quarter, it's much more likely that *every* team member will do their part, and there will be enough food and drink for the entire class to celebrate!

There are other times when conflict—and the resolution—is not so straightforward and easy to solve. Let's say for the class's next celebratory party, two team members decide it's a great idea to order pizza for the class—up the snack ante. But when they bring up this idea, another team member says that you can't order pizza; how are you even going to keep it warm until it's time for class? They suggest sub sandwiches from the local deli because it's a healthier option. But then another team member points out that not everyone likes sandwiches. Besides, some people are gluten free, and there are no good vegetarian sandwich options from that deli, so *actually*, it would be better to order the to-go "Build Your Own Taco" buffet from the Mexican restaurant down the road because that's more fun anyway.

Suddenly, everyone who wants pizza wonders (loudly) why tacos are such a good idea; if tacos can be kept warm, why can't pizza? And then your friend reminds you that they *really* want to bring in their mom's homemade hummus because everyone wants to try it . . . and on and on and on until chaos erupts, people are arguing, and the entire point of the celebration seems to be lost.

You might be tempted to look around the room for the teacher to weigh in, but they've given *you* this responsibility—you are the student leader, so you need to step in and handle the conflict. Even though some (if not most) of the people might not be happy with the ultimate decision, someone does need to step in to help make that ultimate decision. Otherwise, you'll end up with five different meal options—or nothing at all if people get frustrated and choose not to participate.

Your job as the leader is *not* to make sure everyone agrees; remember that we can all "agree to disagree" (I use this phrase often when I lead, and so will you). Keep in mind that as a leader, you're seeking consensus (that people will go along with the decision) rather than agreement (that everyone gets exactly what they want). The more (most?) important point here is for you to address potential—or obvious—disgruntlement, which is conflict. Then, everyone can go back to celebrating how hard you've all worked to earn this party!

A: ASK FOR INPUT

You do not need to know everything about everything to be a leader because you have access to *the* most amazing resource: all the people around you. When you ask for input (other people's ideas) as you make decisions, you become a stronger—and more inclusive!—leader. You become the leader who people want to be around because you are going to ask them what they think. And I have yet to come across a person who does not have an opinion; every time I have asked people for input, they have had things to say. Asking for someone's input shows that you respect them and empowers them as members of the team; this, in turn, creates respect for you as a leader.

And let's be honest: It also allows people to give you insight into what is actually happening in their world. While you are leading and making decisions for the big picture, they are working and thinking about things on the ground level. If the decision will impact them, they want—and will even expect—to have input.

I think asking for input is one of the best and most important parts of being a leader. I've always made it my goal to have people on my team (or those around me in my circle of influence) who know more than I do about various components of our work. This is far from threatening; in fact, it is encouraging! As the leader, I can get their input as needed, and they know I will make the best decision possible for the team to keep us moving forward.

Let's say, for example, that you're in school, and the teacher announces that the class will be building bridges in groups using only toothpicks and glue. She then explains that the goal will be to build the bridge that holds the most amount of weight.

Now, if this had been me back in high school—before I knew about the importance of asking for input—I'd be sinking into the background as much as possible given that I have zero talent for bridge building. But when it comes time for the teacher to choose the team leaders, imagine that she points to you. As the chosen leader, you *definitely* want to ask for input from your teammates as you design the bridge—especially if you're like me, whose brain has no aptitude for engineering principles. But even if you feel totally confident that you could build the entire bridge on your own, you should still stop and ask for ideas. Everyone on the team will have a different perspective, especially if you're all *actually* engineering students, which could bring a new and possibly better idea—or at least spark one.

Asking for input is the way you source insight and knowledge from your team, but it's also a way to build support and trust among the people you are leading. If you want your team to back your decision as a leader, actively seek opportunities for them to provide input. Ask where the toothpicks should go!

R: RESPECT OTHERS

Leaders have the wonderful opportunity to treat people how they would like to be treated and be a role model for others. A core tenet of treating others well is giving respect. When you ask someone a question, respect their time and insight by taking the time to really listen to their answer. Respect someone's contribution to a project by thanking them for a job well done. Show respect and consideration for a team member by first considering what they are currently working on or stressed about *before* you ask them to take on anything more.

Respect is a two-way street. If you want to be respected as a leader, you must show respect to those around you. Then, just watch as the positive impact of mutual respect ripples throughout your group and, ultimately, your work together. You'll be amazed at how quickly respect can help others feel valued and seen. You will also be amazed at how quickly this feeling can be eroded if respect is not consistent. Show people respect, and they will show up for you—every time.

K: KEEP THEIR WORD

Do what you say you are going to do. It's as simple as that.

Actions always speak louder than words. And leaders? They keep their word. So when you say you will do something—find an answer to a question, help a colleague or friend, research the history prompt, buy the book the team needs, ask the professor, contact the newspaper reporter, etc.—do it.

I know many professionals, myself included, who consider a handshake an agreement more binding than a contract. When I offer you my hand,

I extend to you my word. And my word is grounded in respect, both for you and for the agreement we have discussed. My word—my promise—is also supported by the respect I have for myself as a leader and my personal integrity. When you follow through on a promise, you demonstrate that you can be trusted and respected. We've all been around people who said they were going to do something and then did not do it. Don't be that person. Commit. Follow through. Keep your word.

JUMP BACK INTO THE OCEAN

The stereotypical shark, the carpet shark, the sawshark, and the other 500+ species of sharks—they all share five defining traits.

And the countless types of leaders—the experienced leader, the new leader, the supercharged leader, and each other kind of leader—they, too, all share five defining traits.

So when you're in any kind of leadership role that inevitably becomes overwhelming, simply come back to this Leadership Tale about the SHARK. Dial back into the five defining traits that all leaders share:

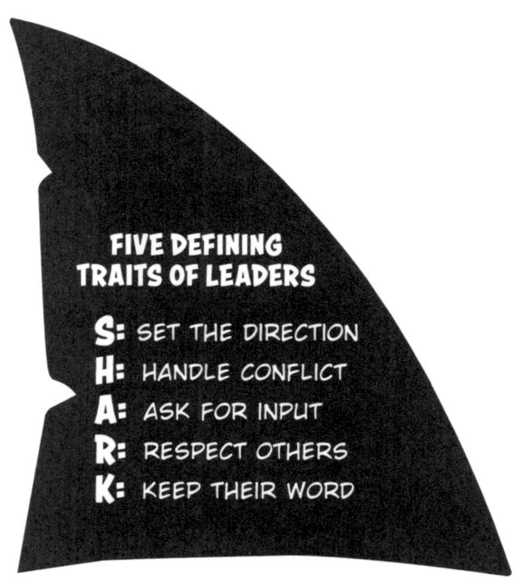

These will help guide you back to what you should *do* as a leader, which in turn will help remind you of who you *are* as a leader.

Then jump back into your leadership ocean. You've got this.

Tasman: Sharks are awesome. I wrote my college essay about the various experiences I've had with sharks, either in the wild or at an aquarium. I love telling people all about my shark encounters because it provides the much-needed perspective that sharks are not man-eating beasts. They are really quite beautiful, and each one is unique. (I will let you draw your own conclusions about leadership from this.)

Kepler: Of all the characteristics that leaders share, I think asking for input is probably one of the hardest things for people, especially if they have some sort of authority. A lot of the time, they might feel like it would undermine that authority if they ask someone else for help or input. But if a leader can't communicate to their team that there's a problem and ask their team for help, then whatever the leader is trying to accomplish will be greatly hindered. My art teacher is my favorite teacher because she consistently asks for our input and listens to our ideas. That's what makes me respect her authority even more.

LEADERSHIP IN REAL LIFE

Long before I was running summer programs at renowned aquariums and writing books on leadership, I was a senior in college and working as an intern at the zoo. There, I was offered the enormous opportunity—and responsibility—to plan a weekend zoo event for families. I jumped right in and began sifting through every detail while simultaneously trying to keep the big picture in mind. I also had to motivate other zoo employees and volunteers to work hard during what I knew would be an insanely busy two days in the oppressive heat of summer.

The first morning of the event, the other people who were helping to set up and run the event began arriving on schedule, and everyone could feel the excitement was in the air . . . except one volunteer, who was stomping right toward me with a scowl on their face.

"Who's in charge around here?" they demanded.

"That would be me," I said with a proud smile. "How can I help?"

"Well, I did *not* receive my parking pass *or* my directions," the angry volunteer said, "and now I have *no* idea what to do with my car!" They nodded in the direction of the busy street in front of the zoo entrance, where their car was idling in a no-parking zone.

"I sent the pass and directions two weeks ago," I said calmly.

Their eyes narrowed. "No, you most certainly did not."

"Yes, I assure you," I responded. "I sent all the passes and directions out at once."

Their voice raised another octave and another decibel as they reiterated that they had *no* pass and *no* instructions.

I countered their increase in volume and intensity and explained once again that, yes, I had sent the pass and directions, so perhaps *they* had missed seeing it or simply forgot.

As you might have guessed, not only did this fail to end the conflict, but it also had the very real (and very quick) consequence of

CONTINUED →

making it much, much worse. We were both mad, and we were both getting louder.

Here it was, only 8:30 a.m., and things were already going wrong. Was this person really questioning my leadership skills? During my first big event at the zoo?

My boss suddenly appeared at my side with a parking pass extended in her hand, calmly explained where to park, and thanked the volunteer so very much for coming to help.

Immediately, the volunteer's shoulders visibly relaxed. They smiled, thanked my boss, and scurried back to their car to get supplies to help prep for the big event.

I was still furious. As soon as the person was out of earshot, I turned to my boss and explained that I had absolutely, for sure followed through and sent everything to everyone. I was worried that my boss would think the mix-up was my fault. I was upset that the other person seemed to get their way. And I was mad that I didn't know what else to do.

My boss held her hand up, and I stopped defending myself. She explained that handling the conflict in the moment was much more important than who was right or wrong. Then, she patted my shoulder and said, "Now we have an event to throw. Let's go have some fun and make sure everyone else does too."

My boss had dealt with the situation, resolved the conflict, and now we were moving on to have a great day.

Leadership lesson learned.

LEADERSHIP FIELD NOTES

- Think about the five defining traits explained through the acronym SHARK, and pick the one you feel most confident about. Then, write down two concrete ways in which you bring this trait to life.
- Consider which SHARK trait is challenging for you, and write down two scenarios that prove your point.
- For the trait you feel confident about, can you actively seek out ways to role model and support others as they are learning this trait? For the trait that is challenging for you, think of a trusted friend, teacher, coach, or other person who does this well, and ask if they can provide feedback on how you can improve this skill.

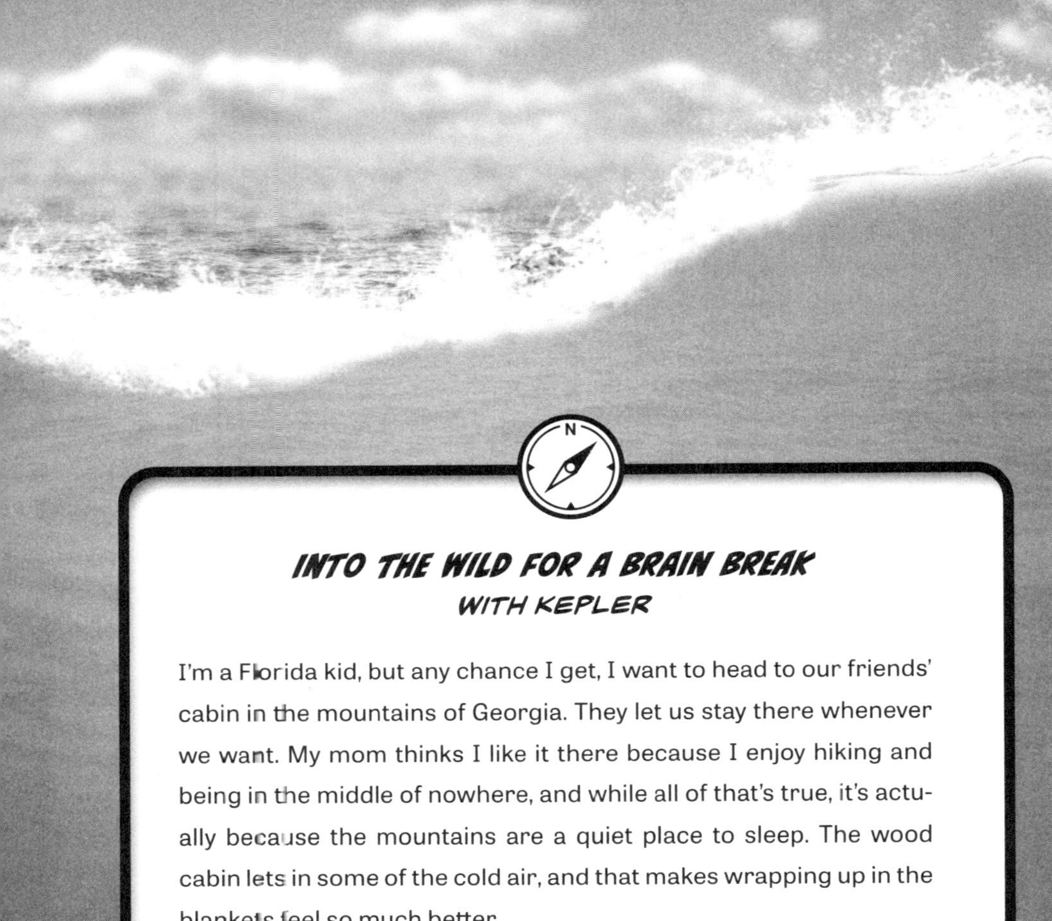

INTO THE WILD FOR A BRAIN BREAK
WITH KEPLER

I'm a Florida kid, but any chance I get, I want to head to our friends' cabin in the mountains of Georgia. They let us stay there whenever we want. My mom thinks I like it there because I enjoy hiking and being in the middle of nowhere, and while all of that's true, it's actually because the mountains are a quiet place to sleep. The wood cabin lets in some of the cold air, and that makes wrapping up in the blankets feel so much better.

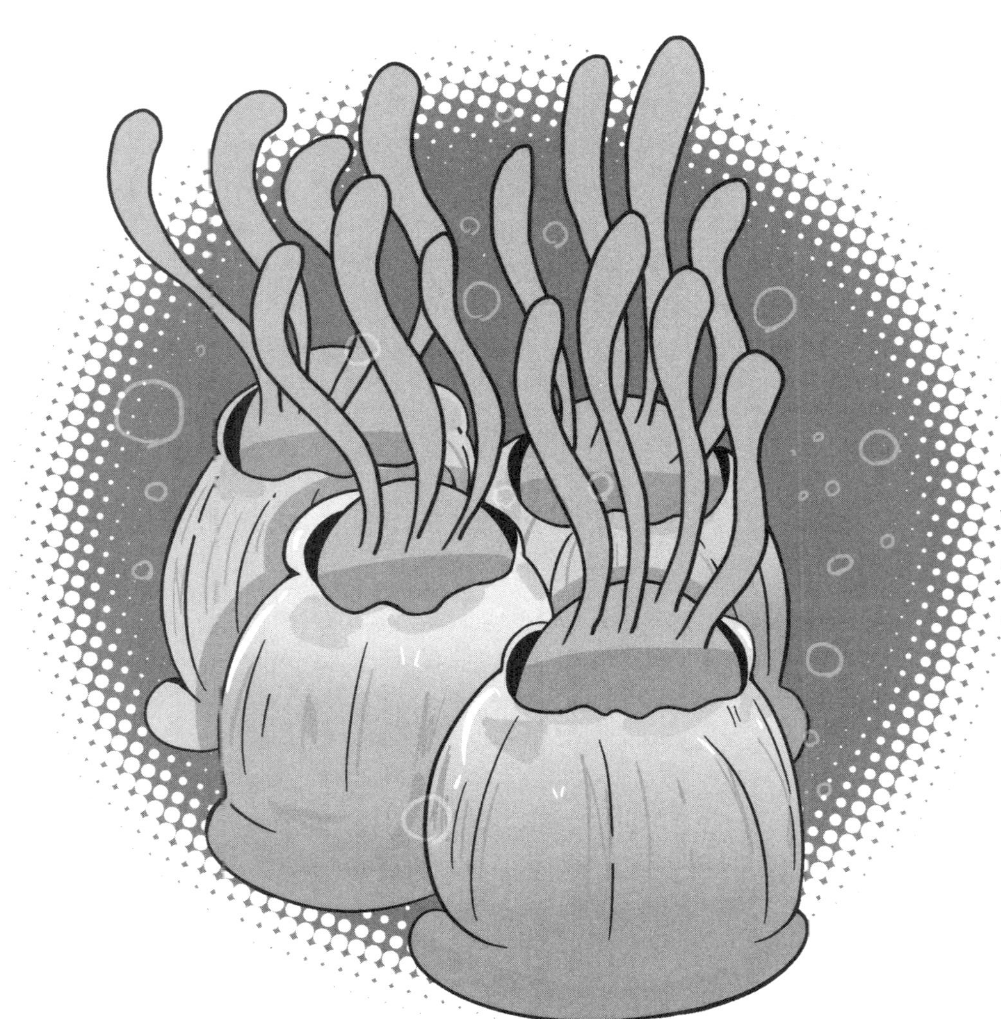

LEADERSHIP TALE #3

YOU WERE BUILT TO FAIL AS WELL AS SUCCEED

(READY FOR THE NEXT WAVE? THE BARNACLES ARE)

"I have failed many times many times in my life. But more importantly, I've learned from every setback, proudly own up to my mistakes, grown from disappointments, and now I'm . . . ready for the runway."

—ADAM RIPPON, OLYMPIC FIGURE SKATER

I am that mom who's forever concocting adventures for my two teenagers. Usually, they're the types of family vacations that require lots of travel—different modes of travel, all hours of the day and night. Thankfully, over the years, Tasman and Kepler have learned to play along. Or maybe they've just *decided* to since any trip offers pretty cool experiences that they couldn't get at home. Recently, they informed me that what we're actually doing is going on a bunch of side quests. Regardless, they've definitely mastered the ability to (more or less) hide any eye-rolling or otherwise incredulous expressions on their faces when I remind them along the journey to "smile because we're *making family memories*!"

This is how, a while back, we found ourselves driving down a never-ending highway, thousands of miles from home, delirious with exhaustion, and working hard to keep any impatience at bay until we reached our destination. Then I started singing—at the top of my lungs.

You might think this is the moment the eye-rolling became over the top and audible groans emerged from every part of the car. But in all the travel craziness of the day, this was the moment my teens expected to emerge after the last few hours of controlled chaos.

And so I continued singing, with Kepler and Tasman gradually joining in on the parts they knew, until Kepler interrupted us all to announce, "You know, Mom, I'm pretty sure we're the only family driving down the road singing a song about barnacles."

FROM LEADER*SHIP* TO LEAD*ING*

The first two Leadership Tales were all about leader*ship*: understanding what it is, what we all have in common as leaders, and what makes you unique as a leader. It's time to now move from leader*ship* as a concept to lead*ing* as an action. There's plenty more I could teach you about the concept of leadership (and plenty more you will learn along your journey), but it's time to stop talking about it and start doing it.

What is leader*ship* all about?

Making decisions. One decision at a time.

So what is lead*ing* all about?

Failing.

Ouch. Feels a bit harsh, right? Let me soften the edge a bit.

What else is leading all about?

Succeeding!

Let's get onto a virtual basketball court for a minute.

For every basketball you swish or free throw you make during the game, you've missed thousands in practice (and probably during a game too). The difference? During practice, the audience is smaller, expectations are less, there's (usually)no score on the scoreboard, and there's definitely no season at stake.

During the game, all the expectations can feel like a ton of bricks on your shoulders. You take a deep breath, focus your energy, and trust your training. It's all you can do in the moment; sometimes it works, and sometimes it doesn't. Sometimes you succeed, and sometimes you fail. When everyone is watching and your teammates are counting on you to make the shot, not making it can feel soul crushing.

Failing at leadership feels like missing a free throw during a crucial basketball game. When you've spent countless hours learning how to lead, getting to know your teammates, deciding what decision you want to make, and then actually making that decision, it can feel like you let everyone down even though you were trying to make the best decision you could. Your teammates could seem (or even really be) mad at you even though you had the best intentions at heart.

But if you're going to commit to leading, you have to commit to failing. It is absolutely impossible to always make the right decision, one that everyone will agree with, a decision that will always result in the outcome you were targeting, or one that will be celebrated. The sooner you resolve to understand that you will fail as a leader, the sooner you will start actually leading.

FROM BASKETBALL TO BARNACLES

I love the game of basketball. It's exciting, fast-paced, and full of possibilities. I was a cheerleader in high school for our team, and now Tasman has evolved to being an uber-fan of the game. But neither of us is good at playing the sport. No matter how hard we try or how many lessons we receive, we are much better at cheering from the periphery than we are at attempting to play.

But barnacles . . . these animals intrigue us as much as the game of basketball does . . . *and* we can get in close and observe them as well as watch them from afar. Where can you find barnacles? Everywhere from tidepools to the bottom of boats. They may look like they're more rock with a hole in the middle than they are animal, but they are an animal nonetheless. The animal builds a rock-like shell around itself, then lives its life with its head glued to a firm surface. When they are hungry, they stick their wispy legs out into the sea and catch some plankton drifting by. They do this repeatedly throughout the day and night until the tide goes out and they find themselves literally out of the water for what could be hours on end.

Barnacles are tidal animals, which means sometimes they are in the ocean (during high tide), and sometimes they are not in the water at all (during low tide). They have to be ready for the harsh reality that even though they need to be in the water to survive, at times during the day or night, they will not be. Sometimes, they will feel like they've got it all together, comfy in the water, reaching the pinnacle of barnacle success—what I equate with feeling successful as a leader and making good decisions that everyone is on board with. But sometimes, they will feel like a fish (actually an invertebrate) out of water—because they actually will be.

If you feel like you are failing as a leader, you can feel like a fish out of water too: All your creature comforts are gone, and you're faced with some harsh realities.

The good news? The next tide is just around the corner—bringing nourishment and life support. The reality? It could be minutes or hours, but it is coming. Just like your next decision as a leader is just around the corner.

HERE COMES YOUR NEXT FAILURE!

Ugh. Not exactly the result I was hoping for.

I figure all leaders would rather succeed every time, just as I imagine a barnacle would prefer to stay covered by ocean water than deal with the harsh reality of sunlight and a whole new host of land predators, like crabs.

But if you fail as a leader, the time will come again in the not-too-distant future for you to try again. You will step up to the free-throw line in the game or up to the decision-making line in leadership. You might feel nervous, swayed by the crowd, excited about the opportunity, and fearful about the outcome.

The most important part of this moment is leaning into the truth that you were built to fail as well as succeed. The worst thing you can do in the moment isn't missing the shot or making a decision that results in an outcome you don't want. The worst action you can take is to walk away—to choose not to even try to make the shot or make a decision. The worst possible action? No action at all.

Failure is part of the game. It's part of the journey of being a leader.

Tides are part of how the ocean operates. It's part of the lifecycle of a barnacle. There is a popular saying: "Where your attention goes, your energy flows." This is true in school, in sports, in yoga, in business, in life in general: If any of your attention is focused on failing—or even on *not* failing—you are sending energy in the direction of failure too. Not only does this drain you of energy, but it also doesn't prevent failure from occurring. Failure will still come, just like the tide.

So instead, redirect your attention solely to the decision. Then, your energy can flow more positively into making the best decision you can. By committing to make a decision, you commit to fail. But that's OK! Because by committing to fail, you commit to the natural cycle of the tide.

Take the following examples:

- A youth conductor selects a piece of music for the choir that they think will be challenging yet beautiful to sing—but then, during the performance, the harmonies are off, and the crowd reacts to the performance with what seems like half-hearted applause.
- A student is in charge of stocking supplies for the classroom's 3D printer and orders from a new vendor, but when the supplies arrive, the quality is awful. Ultimately, the project the class is working on isn't as good as it should be, *and* it's turned in late because everyone had to fix the problem.
- The leader of the high school science club checks the weather forecast and sees a small chance of rain but still decides to take

everyone outside anyway—including all the excited elementary science club kids who showed up that day to help—to clean up trash in the schoolyard. Suddenly, there's a downpour of rain.

In each of these examples, the leader's focus and energy were on the outcome and direction they had set as the leader. They didn't set out to make a decision that would result in (a perceived) failure. When you lead, you will set out to simply make a decision, which means taking a chance that you might fail. But you also might succeed.

Making decisions *is* leadership, and people depend on you as a leader for that. They are also watching *how* you lead, the chances you take, and the awareness you have that each decision may not go according to plan. As you make bold decisions as a leader, you never know who might be watching and who you could positively influence. Maybe someone is so afraid to fail that they feel paralyzed in making almost any decision, but after watching your decisiveness, they can feel their confidence grow. You will also be a leadership role model when you acknowledge a failure.

And you *will* fail. We all do. You will also succeed. Just as the tides will come and go as they are supposed to, you will fail and succeed as you are supposed to.

When this idea feels scary or uncomfortable, try to picture the barnacles who thrive among the comings and goings of the tide. Then, remember that you, leader, were built for this too.

Me: What is your reaction when I tell you that you are going to fail as a leader?

Tasman (making a face): Ouch. That's really depressing. When it happens, it's a really awful feeling. Failing is a part of leadership, but I hate not being good at things. I think it's necessary, but it totally sucks. I'm used to it, but I still hate it.

Me: What is your reaction when I tell you that you are going to fail as a leader?

Kepler: I knew that. It's not just a part of leadership; it's a part of life. You're going to fail at everything eventually. You can succeed, but you're also going to fail. If something is not going well, just fix it. If you mess up, do the next thing better. Just make the next decision.

LEADERSHIP IN REAL LIFE

I used to start every team meeting or coaching session by talking about wins. I would ask the people I was leading to tell me about their personal wins: the decisions they were most proud of, projects they were working on that were going well, or new ideas they were super excited about. Then, I realized I was missing a crucial piece: We needed to hear about, talk about, support, and celebrate *failure* as well. Failures meant people were thinking big, pushing boundaries, and taking chances. And sharing their failures meant they felt safe enough and confident enough to talk about them.

This was not an easy transition. Most people much prefer talking about what is going well and what they are proud of. But in my groups and sessions, I started to see glimmers of realness. People would relax their shoulders, and I would hear long exhales as they began to trust that I really meant what I said: I wanted to create a safe space for people to feel comfortable talking about how they'd messed up, where decisions had not gone according to plan, when they hadn't been the leader they wanted to or could be.

I *still* work to create this space for myself. Tasman and Kepler help me: They listen and don't rush to judgment when I talk about things I didn't do as well as I could have or decisions I made that I wish I could take back. But then, we talk about the reality of failure, whether on a test, in the arena, or in front of the room. Failure is feedback. How we use that is up to us.

LEADERSHIP FIELD NOTES

- Acknowledge that failure is a part of leadership (just like success), and make this a normal thing to talk about—just like you do for every success that you experience.
- Resolve to be your own biggest champion, and cheer yourself on when you fail.
- When you see your leader fail, resist the urge to criticize or think about how you could have done it better if you had been leading. Choose to remember that you both are working toward the same goal and that failure is a part of the journey—which means they will be able to lead more effectively if they know they have a safe space in which to fail.

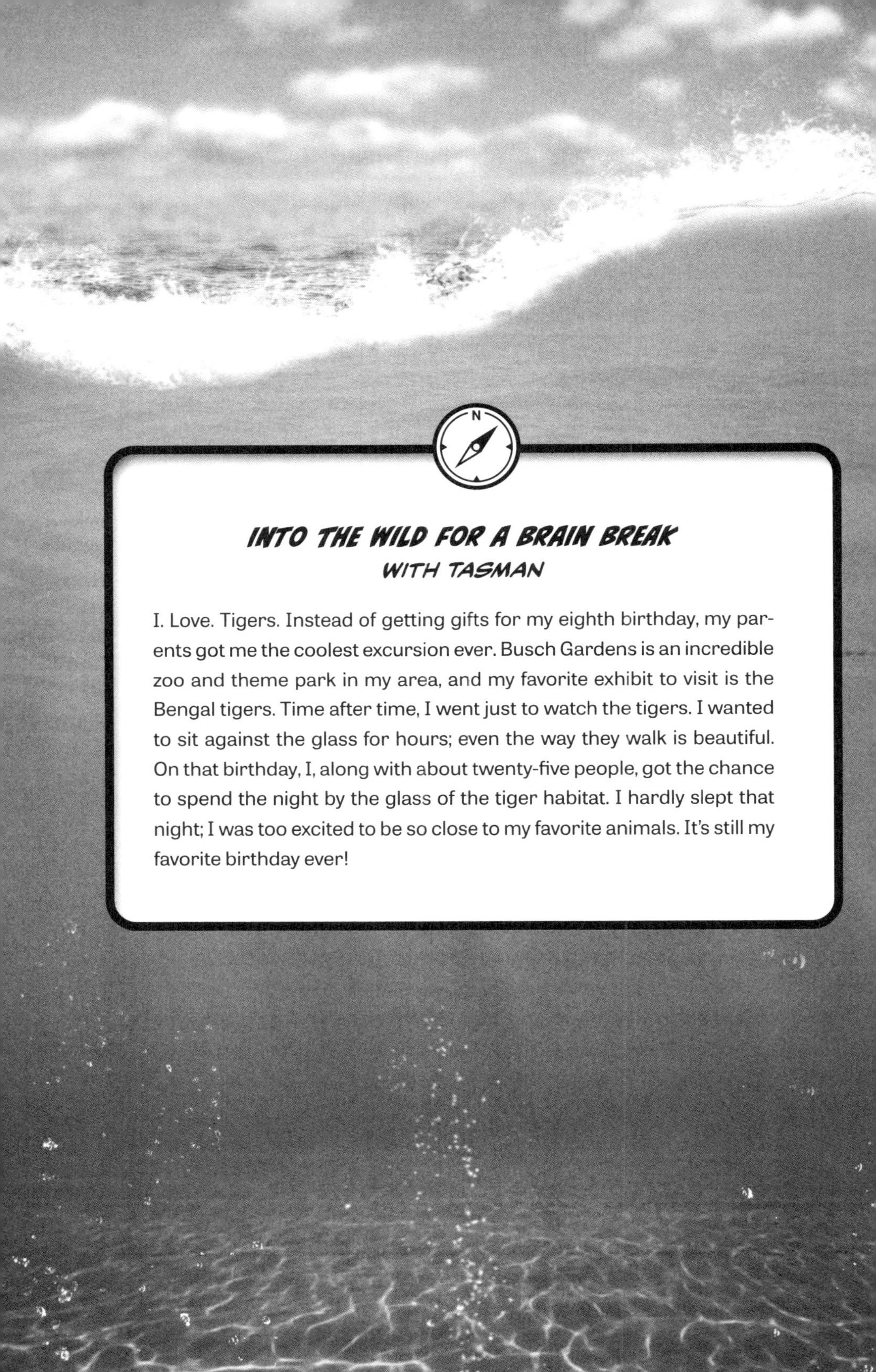

INTO THE WILD FOR A BRAIN BREAK
WITH TASMAN

I. Love. Tigers. Instead of getting gifts for my eighth birthday, my parents got me the coolest excursion ever. Busch Gardens is an incredible zoo and theme park in my area, and my favorite exhibit to visit is the Bengal tigers. Time after time, I went just to watch the tigers. I wanted to sit against the glass for hours; even the way they walk is beautiful. On that birthday, I, along with about twenty-five people, got the chance to spend the night by the glass of the tiger habitat. I hardly slept that night; I was too excited to be so close to my favorite animals. It's still my favorite birthday ever!

LEADERSHIP TALE #4

LOCKING HORNS WITH RESILIENCE JUST MAKES YOU MORE TIRED

(GAME ON, BIGHORN SHEEP)

"At the end of the day, we're human, too, so we have to protect our mind and our body rather than just go out there and do what the world wants us to do."

—SIMONE BILES, OLYMPIC AND WORLD CHAMPION GYMNAST

I will travel as much as I can, any chance I can get. I love exploring, finding adventure, meeting people, discovering new food, and, of course, seeing any wildlife or wild places that I have never seen before. So when three dear friends of mine suggested we meet up for a girls' trip in Las Vegas, I was thrilled. Not only is the city of Las Vegas exciting for a lot of expected reasons—unique hotels, inventive and delicious food, "How did they do that?" magic shows, mind- and body-bending circus acts, street performers, and roller coasters and ziplines in the middle of the city—but there is also the unmistakable allure of the wildlife and wild places just beyond the city limits, waiting to be explored.

So while most people may flock to Las Vegas to see sights such as the 1,000+ water fountains dancing to music and lights outside the Bellagio hotel (which really is amazing to see), I want to venture into the surrounding ecosystem, where there is actually very little water. I want to head out into the desert. The desert ecosystem surrounding Las Vegas seems like an entirely different planet compared with the hustle and bustle of the city.

Even though Las Vegas is also in the desert, in the city, people have gone to great lengths to grow green grass and create water fountains. In the real desert, without as much human intervention, it is an experience all its own. And as temperatures fluctuate between extreme highs and extreme lows, combined with a seeming (or true) lack of water, the plants and animals that have evolved to thrive in this habitat are certainly unique—perhaps even quirky—compared with those we usually find living in our backyards.

After a couple of days of exciting rides, shows, and food, I was beyond thrilled to be driving away from the bright lights and big city of Vegas and heading toward Valley of Fire State Park. Chatting away to my friends as we drove along, I felt like I had only blinked my eyes and, suddenly, the cityscape had been replaced by towering formations of brightly colored earth: Vibrant oranges and reds dominated the landscape, punctuated by swaths of brown and yellow tones. Everywhere I looked brought new images of stark rocky formations, some hundreds of feet in the air, with not a hint of green or blue anywhere to be found.

The talking slowly turned into silence as each one of us stared intently out of our car windows. All of us wildlife enthusiasts were laser focused on soaking up this experience and looking for any evidence of wildlife in this very wild place. Without warning, a barely perceptible movement caught my eye out the window. Transfixed, I immediately placed both hands on the window next to my face so I could stare even more intently where the movement had been—several hundred feet up the side of a rocky formation. As I kept a vigilant watch, I noticed even more movement; then, a handful of hikers appeared in the distance, glaringly obvious with their bright white shirts and black boots, as they followed a very steep path uphill.

I immediately wanted to follow them up the hill, but as we were still driving in our car toward the state park, I resolved to continue my observations. I noticed more movement in a few places along the mountainside. Sometimes, the movement included more hiking boots, brightly colored backpacks, and big floppy hats, with hiking poles being used to stabilize themselves along the path. But some movement did not . . .

If I wasn't watching hikers walk carefully up the side of a steep hill, what was I watching?

Then, suddenly, I realized this unclaimed movement of what I thought were hikers in a very precarious situation on the edge of an almost-vertical drop was not of hikers at all; it was of relatively large animals walking nimbly yet confidently along the path. Any slight adjustment left or right by even a centimeter would most likely send a person crashing down the steep slope or smoosh them against the mountainside. But the animals seemed entirely unbothered by the inherent precariousness of navigating rocky cliffs at heights that made my palms sweat.

Unlike the hikers I had observed moments earlier, who seemed to be relying on careful foot placement and hiking poles for balance, these creatures simply meandered along their way. They clearly knew instinctively how to navigate their steep and rocky natural habitat, and it was clear no hiker was ever going to be able to follow them; this trail was made by (and for) bighorn sheep.

BALANCE IS NOT YOUR GOAL

I'm going to guess that you have *a lot* going on in your life. You probably have projects, homework, and tests at school. You might have a part-time, full-time, or as-needed job like babysitting that you are working at.

Maybe you have commitments to a sport, art, music, or an after-school club. Maybe your family life has shifted recently, and you're navigating a new normal. Maybe some friendships have changed as you've changed classes, as you've moved schools, or just because you've evolved and grown up. And then someone—with good intentions of course—might ask you, "So what's next? What are your plans after high school/college/university/trade school?" or "What are your plans in this job? Is this what you see yourself doing for the rest of your life?"

Suddenly, you want to scream. Or cry. Or run to the top of the hill and hang out with the bighorn sheep.

Because these are not simple questions to answer. There's so much going on in your life. You're simply trying to keep your head above water.

And then a terrifying thought hits you: If you have all this stuff going on in your head, in your life, and more, then so do all the people around you. Now, as you glance around the room in English class, you notice things a little bit differently, like how the person at the front of the room is chewing on her pencil absentmindedly. *Is she trying to figure out the English prompt your professor just assigned or worrying about the test tomorrow?* Then, you notice the boy sitting next to her who looks like he's falling asleep. *Is he just really bored, or has he been up late with a sick pet all night?*

Then, what if the English professor assigns a group project and selects you as the leader of one of the teams? Both of the students you noticed come your way to join your team. As you all start discussing the tasks at hand, the idea of balance seems a little more personal to you now. As you're trying to figure out how you're going to fit this project into your schedule, as the project leader, you now have to consider how you're going to divvy up responsibilities with the stress your other team members are clearly feeling too.

All of this has happened in your head as you come back to the present moment, still face-to-face with the person who asked you the seemingly simple question about your plans for the next phase of your life. If you felt like screaming a moment ago, now that feeling has only intensified. You realize this because the nice person in front of you seems to notice that you look like you're about to lose it.

As you slowly give in to the inner battle, your fists ball, your face contorts, your breathing rapidly intensifies, and the tears start falling. Your hand flies to your mouth to stifle the cry (or shout) that you want to let loose.

The very nice asker of the innocent question offers you the best advice they can think of in the moment, which might sound something like this: "You know, you really need to just relax; life is all about balance!"

Now you *really* want to scream.

I don't blame you; I would too. Let me jump into this story and stand next to the person who asked you that question, because, yes, you do need to relax at times, but we'll get back to that. More importantly, I want to first let you in on a not-so-secret-but-not-shouted-out-enough reality:

There is no such thing as school–work–life balance.

Every time someone tells you they are working toward a school–work–life balance? Never going to happen. When someone suggests that your New Year's resolutions should include striving for balance in your life to bring happiness and peace? Not possible. The very notion of balance as a goal is wrong from the start because that implies that balance itself is attainable and sustainable, that somehow you can reach the point where everything is in balance and therefore can stay that way, and that there is a point at which it can all be still and calm and you won't need to work toward this goal anymore.

Is that what balance really is—the end goal itself that is endlessly possible?

Think about it. Picture in your head someone who is "balancing," and notice how they maintain their balance. Is every part of them still? If you think about a person on a balance beam, look at their arms: They are constantly moving to maintain balance. If you envision a person on a slack rope or high wire, are they perfectly frozen in time or moving too? What about a person on a snowboard? All of these people are making constant micro (and sometimes macro) adjustments to help them maintain their balance.

When you go to a class to learn any of these skills, what's the first thing they teach you? How to stay perfectly upright without wobbling at all? Nope. They teach you how to fall and get back up safely so you can be ready for the next time. Why? Because the instructor knows that not only is balance not probable forever; it is not possible. Rather than furthering the notion that balance itself is the goal, they recognize that you will fall and you will need to start again. So they teach you how to get up after you fall.

If you strive to balance every part of your life, you have set yourself up to fail. If you are striving to do this as a person *and* as a leader, now you will be falling short in both facets of your life. Let's pretend for a moment that you *do* achieve what you consider to be balance and feel like you've got everything handled; how long do you think this will last?

Maybe until your professor assigns you a new project, and now you feel overwhelmed again? Or you need to learn a new piece of music, and it's just out of your vocal range, so you feel nervous? Or there is a new cash register to train on, and it's the holiday season, so you know that patience will run thin if you don't ring items up the right way the first time? Your tight hold on balance now seems thrown off again—because it is.

It's not that balance is an unworthy goal; it's just the *wrong* goal. Those bighorn sheep I watched climbing up the steep side of a mountain? It's not really that they are perfectly balanced all of the time; it's more about the tiny adjustments and adaptations they have that prepare them for when they're not. If they start to lose their grip on a slippery surface or slide on loose rocks, their hooves can pinch to get a better hold, and they even have claws that act as brakes.[1] Instead of striving for balance and expecting that to be the end result, I invite you to think about the adaptations you already have and shift your focus to something that is far more realistic and sustainable. Instead of balance, your new focus is resilience.

TASMAN'S LEADERSHIP TALE

Working on this book has truly been a collaborative project for me, Kepler, and Tasman. We bounced ideas off each other; discussed realities, opportunities, and challenges they face; and brainstormed the best animals to help us teach these concepts. As we worked through this, I watched how each of my kids responded. Whereas Kepler weighed in when needed and let it go the rest of the time, Tasman would become increasingly interested. Then increasingly invested. Then increasingly engaged to the point that she took this book fully on with all her other responsibilities. I took off my virtual author hat to put on my Mama Julie hat and responded how any parent would: I asked her how things were going.

Immediately, her eyes lit up, her breathing quickened, and her hands started flying around as she loudly and hurriedly told me all the things that she needed to do, how stressed she was, how everything was both urgent and important (therefore all priorities), and that she wasn't sure how to manage it all—but she still loves all of the challenges in her life, wants to see all of her friends, needs to buy ten new books to read, wants to know if she can go to the beach on Saturday, and, even though she feels overwhelmed and doesn't know what to do at times, she wouldn't change a thing because she is driven to succeed, loves the fast pace of life, and even when she crashes at a moment's notice, it's all still fun.

Whew! (And if you read that last run-on paragraph as fast as she spoke it, you are just now coming up for a breath too.)

I followed up her brain dump of overwhelm by explaining my idea for Leadership Tale #4. Her response was immediate and more than a little enthusiastic: "*I need that Leadership Tale!*"

In addition to the realities of her full and fruitful life, Tasman has struggled with mental health challenges over the years. It is with her permission that I share this with you as a way to talk openly about mental health and its impact on us as leaders as well as when we are being led by others. Tasman's mental health struggles have been specific to anxiety and have manifested in everything from intense feelings of out-of-control overwhelm to full-blown panic attacks.

In full disclosure and transparency to keep it real with mental health, I completely identify with Tasman's struggles because these have been my struggles as well. Honestly, I think both Tasman and I need this Leadership Tale as much as some of you. And even if you don't struggle with anxiety, overwhelm, or panic attacks, perhaps this Tale can help you better understand how to support those around you in leadership roles.

So when I tell you that you must reimagine balance in a more achievable way so you can achieve that goal, it is both as a leadership development professional as well as a mother who supports her daughter and struggles with anxiety herself. It is imperative to me that Tasman understands how to separate the intense feelings of anxiety from her natural passionate enthusiasm. One is a mental health reality, and one is part of the fabric of her soul. Both influence how she leads and how she is led—and both can be well served by the principle of resilience.

And thus, this became Tasman's Leadership Tale.

Remember that our goal is not balance; it is resilience. This means our focus is not on the perceived stillness that comes along with balance, but instead, our focus is resilience, which is ultimately about energy management. Everything you do takes energy, and you need to spend as much time recharging after as you do in preparation.

Let's look at the bell curve so you can better visualize what I mean.

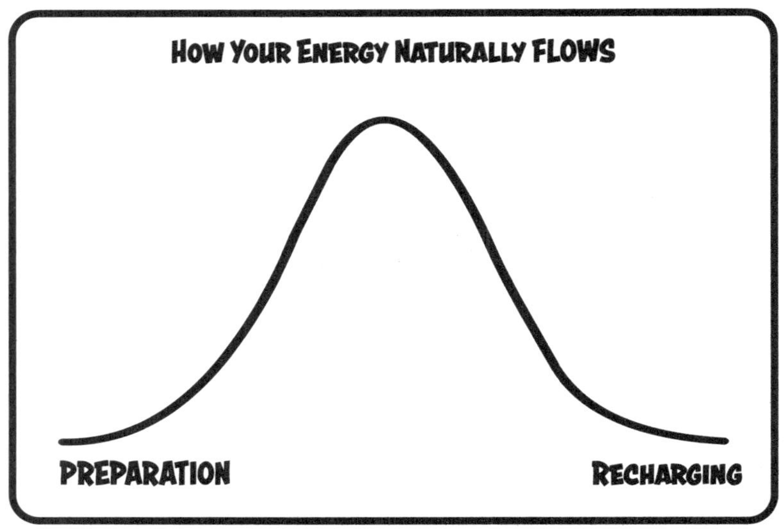

DIAGRAM 2: RESILIENCE BELL CURVE

As you are getting ready for an event (e.g., a presentation, a game, a recital, or a test), you are expending energy. If you are the leader in these scenarios, even more energy is expended in preparation. Then, the event happens (the top of the bell curve). Awesome job—congrats! I'm sure it went amazingly well.

What happens next? Typically, you move on to the next project, the next game, the next anything. I understand why: because everything feels both urgent and important. It can feel impossible to set priorities because you have teachers, coaches, bosses, parents, and others inserting deadlines into your life. With limited control and lots of responsibilities, you could just give in to the chaos.

But instead of surrendering to perceived (or real) chaos, when setting and keeping priorities seems impossible, there is a way to incorporate resilience—energy management—into your life. Notice how the bell curve is just that: a curve. Trust me when I say that energy in your life flows on a bell curve. It will always flow up, peak during your "on" time, and then need to flow down. If you rush onto the next thing and do not allow for the energy to flow down the backside of the curve? It will simply build on itself.

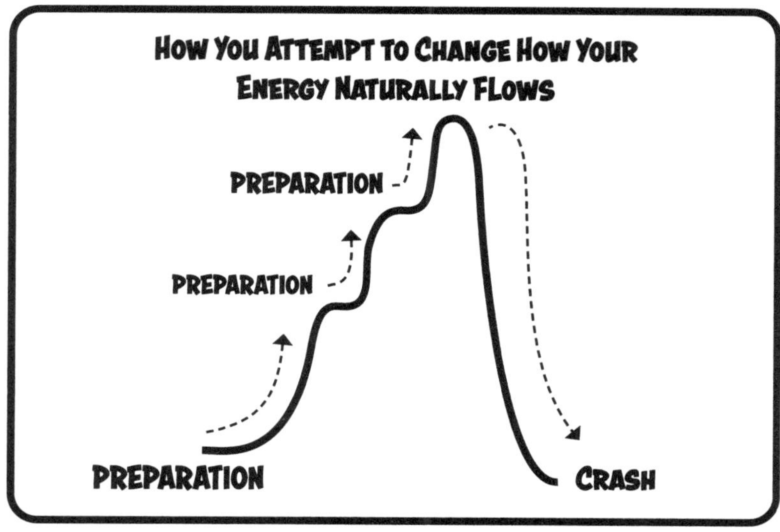

DIAGRAM 3: ENERGY BELL CURVE (WITH OUR ATTEMPTS TO CHANGE IT)

Eventually—maybe not today, maybe not tomorrow, but eventually—your energy will flow back down. You will need that rest-and-recharge part of the bell curve. Does that mean you are always quiet and resting in a hammock? No—but that would be Kepler's choice. Some of you might follow Tasman's lead and head to the local café and bookstore to meet friends. And some of you might need to jump into a large social gathering because that is your rest-and-recharge strategy.

The important point is that you cannot outsmart this part of the bell curve. You can continue to build and build and build while you run from project to project to project, but mark my words that the back end of the bell curve will still occur. The question is not "'if" but "when"—and the more crucial question is how high your bell curve will be before your energy comes crashing down and needs to be replenished.

And if you try to fight this overall? If you don't believe your energy flows on a bell curve? Well, that is like locking horns with a bighorn sheep.

Tasman: I love that this is my Leadership Tale. My brain is a wild place to be. Between ADHD and anxiety, it's easy for me to get overwhelmed; I always seem to have something going on. Recognizing when I need breaks is something I have never been good at, but my mom has taught me that it's something everybody needs to learn, no matter how their mind works.

I am, first and foremost, a science nerd. I can relate just about every law in this book to a concept in either chemistry or physics. When reading Leadership Tale #4 and what my mom wrote about the myth of balance, I was immediately reminded of the misconception surrounding equilibrium. In chemistry, we are taught that equilibrium is what a reaction strives for. The misconception is when people believe a reaction stops occurring once this is achieved. This is entirely false: Equilibrium is reached when the rate of the forward reaction is equal to the rate of the reverse reaction. There is no net change in the concentrations of the reactants and the products over time, yet the reaction never stops occurring. Therefore, even though the movement is unseen, the reaction is not static; it is dynamic.

I am also a circus performer, so I can attest to the fact that in the circus, high-wire walkers move their arms a lot. In fact, hardly any of them walk with nothing in their hands. They all start out with a huge and super heavy pole (some are more than 40 pounds!) held horizontally in order to stay upright. Walking without the pole is shocking to the audience; it's way harder.

Balance is an idea. It's a concept people made up to convince the world that life is perfect. But it's not! We're all on some sort of tightrope. We may alternate walking with the pole or without, but we have to start somewhere. Getting overwhelmed is normal, and learning how to manage it is a skill we can all improve on.

LOCKING HORNS JUST WASTES ENERGY

Of all our Leadership Tales, I believe this is the one that may get the most pushback or seem the most unrelated to the concept of leadership. And that is because when I work with high-performing leaders at every level and age, they grow accustomed to their workload. They adapt to the ever-increasing pace of their expectations—both of themselves and of the people they are leading—in line with the influence and impact they want to have.

In reality, this is a learned behavior. What these leaders are actually doing is simply expanding (growing taller) their resilience bell curve. They are not outlasting, outperforming, or even outsmarting their resilience needs; they are simply extending the height of their bell curve, which increases both the energy expended at the beginning as well as the downturn of energy at the end. What goes up must always come down.

And the moment they try to fight this reality is the moment they—like you—will lock horns with a bighorn sheep.

Both male and female bighorn sheep grow horns. For males, these horns can weigh up to 40 pounds and are designed to help as they compete for dominance, battle for territory, and secure mating rights. Males can run at each other at speeds up to 40 miles per hour, and when they lock horns, the sound can be heard up to a mile away, sounding like an explosion. They can continue these battles for up to twenty-four hours.

I don't know about you, but I have certainly felt those times when I have run full speed at resilience—when I have attempted to push back because I needed to study more for a test, wanted to get ahead on my project, had part of a film to watch before the football game, or was simply interested in researching more before my next interview. Unsurprisingly, resilience pushed back; in fact, it seemed to run at me just as hard. Every time I told myself I was "just going to check email really quickly," resilience reminded me that energy was required for that. Each email I read would elicit an emotional response, regardless of how detached I planned to be.

Even though I want to teach you this exceptionally important concept about resilience, I confess that I have not learned it fully myself. It's easy to slip back into "just five more minutes" or "I'll rest tomorrow." But there is a reason resilience has 40-pound horns too: Without meeting us on an equal playing field, we may never take resilience seriously.

And if you are the leader? The reality of embracing and championing your own energy needs on both sides of the bell curve becomes even more important. You are actively setting a standard, supporting others, and serving as a role model. You cannot tell others to take care of themselves while you neglect your own needs. Your actions carry far more weight than your words, and the people around you are paying attention.

There is an old saying that you have most likely heard, especially if you have ever flown on an airplane: Put your own oxygen mask on first.

If you don't first honor and act on your own energy needs, how do you expect others to do so for their energy needs? And the idea that you want others to take care of themselves first does not hold merit here. If you don't show up as fully healthy and capable as you could be, you cannot support others. You must set yourself up for success before you set others up for success. You must honor the back end of your energy bell curve while you are telling others to honor theirs.

Bighorn sheep do not back down. They are well equipped to survive on the side of a mountain and will lock horns if you come running.

Sounds like quite a lot of energy to me. I'd rather spend my energy working toward my unique influence and impact as a leader and fully embrace my resilience bell curve, because chances are the bighorn sheep aren't changing anytime soon. They will still be found high up on a mountain, somewhere in the desert, living their lives to the fullest.

I see no need to lock horns unnecessarily with resilience and waste precious energy. I think 40 pounds sounds quite heavy to carry around, and producing a sound that can be heard up to a mile away has got to leave me exhausted. I will focus my attention elsewhere and learn to manage my energy.

But just in case I forget and try to outsmart resilience, I'm sure they'll be there to remind me . . .

Game on, bighorn sheep.

Kepler: I think Tasman can go a lot longer than me in a crowd of people that she *doesn't* know, but I can go a substantial amount of time with people I *do* know. You're always supposed to move beyond your limits but know your boundaries so you don't go too far. I try to take the minimum amount of recharge time to operate at my full potential. If I don't take the time to recharge, then I can't show up ready to go. It's kind of like a wind-up toy: If you keep turning and turning and turning it, it's not going to go anywhere. But if you release it at just the right time, then it will go far. It eventually always needs rewinding again, though.

LEADERSHIP IN REAL LIFE

During my third month working at the aquarium, I arrived one morning, preparing myself for the onslaught that the busy summer day would bring. The line of guests already extended out the front doors, down the stairs, around the corner toward the street, and out of sight. I was wearing my most comfortable shoes and had tucked my hair back into a ponytail, ready for a long day of extensive walking, helping, and interacting with guests of all ages and at all spaces throughout the aquarium.

When our daily morning meeting started, we didn't begin with the typical aquarium-wide updates. Instead, one of my team members asked us to make a circle and extend our arms. Soon, they began leading us through breathing exercises, visualizations, and even improvisational games. My inner spirit that craved order fought back: *Why are we wasting our time doing these things when we need to be getting ready for the crowds?* My outer behavior followed along like a supportive member of the team.

Finally, someone else asked why in the world we were wasting our time taking deep breaths and visualizing when we could be focusing on things that actually needed to get done?

Without missing a beat, my team member responded without a hint of offense or anger at the question, only with directness and purpose: The day was about to overtake us with busyness, and our energy was about to be spent. Our role was to be present for the guests we were about to welcome—and since 2.2 million of them visited annually, there was a high chance we'd have a large crowd today. Not only was this moment of calm important; it was imperative.

I'm not sure I believed this, but I went along anyway. Yet as the day went on, I really did feel my energy shift as I continued to meet with the crowds and deliver messages in the moment. And at the end of the day, I felt more centered than drained. I was converted.

LEADERSHIP FIELD NOTES

- At the beginning of the week, mentally think through all of your responsibilities and time commitments. Ask yourself, *How can I best set myself up for success?* Identify a concrete answer (e.g., what time you want to be done with homework or reading each night), and hold yourself accountable (e.g., put an alarm on your phone, or ask your roommate to check in on you).
- Become aware of the early signs of anxiety: Is your heart rate increasing? Is your breathing getting shallower? Are your hands sweating? Are you pacing around the room? When these occur, first reassure yourself that you have your own back, and then act accordingly: Leave the room, turn off the phone, shut your eyes, or simply sit in stillness. Do all of this unapologetically as the leader that you are.
- Make resilience a normal part of conversations when you ask others how they are doing. If they share they are stressed, acknowledge that, and actively listen so you can support them.

INTO THE WILD FOR A BRAIN BREAK
WITH KEPLER

Drinking rock juice. Got your attention? Great. We went on a sea kayaking trip in Channel Islands National Park off the coast of California and got to go to a bunch of caves that were previously inhabited by the Chumash people. The caves had all kinds of cool art painted by Indigenous people on the walls, but in one cave, the coolest thing was that part of the rock was eternally spewing out a little stream of water. We got to kayak next to it—which was actually really difficult to do in a mostly dark cave with waves—and the rock was basically a natural water fountain. Although the water tasted like minerals, it was still a cool and memorable experience.

LEADERSHIP TALE #5

EMPATHY IS A LEADERSHIP SUPERPOWER

(FROM GROWING CACTI TO HERDING CATS)

"Just because someone stumbles and loses their path doesn't mean they're lost forever. Sometimes, we all need a little help."

—PROFESSOR X, *X-MEN: DAYS OF FUTURE PAST*

Many years ago, when Tasman was turning six, we had her birthday party at a local park. All of her friends came screaming out of the cars and ran excitedly toward the swings. The parents meandered along after and joined me at the picnic tables for snacks and drinks to cool us off from the hot day. After hours of play, cake eating, present opening, and many rounds of singing "Happy Birthday," the party was coming to an end, and it was time for the most dreaded part (in my mind): providing gifts to the attendees.

I've always hated the idea of providing take-home gifts at a birthday party, mostly because it usually involves random plastic toys that would be played with for a hot minute before most likely ending up in a closet, under a bed, in the donation bag, or in the trash bag bound for the landfill. It just didn't fit with our environmental—or sustainable-friendly—family values to do this, so I went rogue. Instead of the customary bags filled with plastic or candy, I brought out Tasman's party favors: a tray filled with mini-cacti.

Within seconds, a myriad of six-year-old hands started grabbing at will their chosen cactus.

I guess I should have thought about the fact that I was giving plants with a multitude of literal sharp edges to a bunch of first graders, whose parents may or may not have been on board with this idea. But honestly, it never even crossed my mind that they would not appreciate this gift, because in my house, this would have been awesome—a plant that I could actually keep alive and no abundance of plastic! And then I looked at the parents' faces . . .

They were not thrilled. In fact, some of them were downright horrified as their children came running toward our tray full of pointy plants.

Most of them recovered quickly, and they stepped up to help their child pick out their chosen cactus. I think a few even mumbled "thank you" on the way to their car. I did see more than a few looks of glee on the faces of the kids.

Our birthday party may not have been the most posted about on social media that day. Or maybe it was, but not necessarily to celebrate my daughter; they could have been calling out our random party favor. Yet all I remember in the aftermath was Tasman's face of pure joy and feeling proud of myself for selecting such a creative and unique party favor, one that was truly representative of my daughter. I'm not sure if that sentiment was shared by anyone else.

It's true that you can never actually walk a mile in another person's shoes, although that's what we are encouraged to do to make a connection. I'll never really understand another person's journey, although I will always be interested in their story. And although our cacti may not have been the most appreciated party favor, it may have been for reasons completely unknown to me. Perhaps the parents were afraid that their young children would injure themselves on the pointy bits since they had a habit of doing that. Maybe they couldn't keep plants alive very well either (like me), so now they felt like they were going to fail as a parent. They could have an animal at home that might interact poorly with the cactus, and they didn't have the money to take it to the vet. Or there could have been a whole host of other reasons.

In selecting a cactus as a party favor, I was certainly introducing (or even forcing) our family values in the most innocuous of settings: a six-year-old's birthday party. Suddenly, my eclectic choice felt far heavier than it had to be. Truly, I just wanted to stop giving plastic.

Then, recently, a young (millennial) person shared with me, "For my generation, pets are the new children, and plants are the new pets."

Many of you reading this book may be Gen Z or millennials, so perhaps you can identify with this statement. Maybe I wasn't that far off after all.

Cactus, anyone?

THE "SOFT" SIDE OF LEADERSHIP

Of all the things I've heard during my years of working with leaders, there is one notion that makes me exceptionally frustrated (and maybe even downright mad): the idea that leadership skills are "soft" skills. Somehow, we spend a lot of time, money, and energy training and reinforcing how to do the technical piece of a job or the nuts-and-bolts piece of a project. But then we seem to forget that it is a *person* who is being asked to do something or contribute to the big picture. Even worse, when you are good at doing the job, many times, you then get promoted or asked to be the leader. But the training on *how* to lead? Or the *time* to learn how to do it? That is not always as front and center as the job to do or the project to work on.

Leadership skills are often referred to as "soft" skills, but I would like to offer a different term: They are "essential" skills. And front and center of these leadership skills is how to get to know the people you are leading.

Have you ever decided to move a club meeting to a new day without realizing that some of your club members had a bunch of tests on that same day? Have you been so busy working hard making decisions for the team that you didn't realize your teammate's dog was critically ill? Or have you asked someone to work on a piece of the project because you thought they already had the experience, only to realize that you had completely stressed them out because they had no idea what they were doing?

As you are building relationships as the leader and working to earn trust, a core strategy to do that is to actually know the people you are leading. Some questions you could ask are the following:

- Are you an introvert, extrovert, or somewhere in between?
- What positions do you like to play on the field?
- How long have you been playing your instrument?
- Why did you start learning how to draw?
- What makes you slightly nervous?
- What makes you super uncomfortable and may even lead you to quit the project?
- Do you like feedback in a straightforward way and to your face, or would you prefer it in writing so you have time to digest it before talking about it?
- Do you like this class and want to know more, or are you just passing time?
- Do you have an innate fear of public speaking, yet it's a requirement for our project?
- Are you ultra-confident and wish you were the leader even though it's someone else's role?

If you're going to ask them to trust your decisions and believe in your vision, you will have a far better chance of getting them to agree if they feel like you are talking directly to them—as individual people—rather than to a generic group.

You want to be seen as your own person and your own leader, right? The people you are leading do too; they want to be truly seen for who they are. As you get to know more about them—what makes them tick—you will start to recognize and value new ways in which they can contribute to your project, team, etc. Then, your team becomes stronger and more cohesive as you charge forth toward your goals.

FRIENDSHIP VERSUS EMPATHY

Wait a minute. You might be thinking something along the lines of, *This is sounding suspiciously like building friendships. I don't want to necessarily become friends with everyone I'm leading. In fact, I've been told that I should not do this because then I might become conflicted when making decisions or even be tempted to play favorites. I need to be as objective as possible so I can remain focused on the task or project at hand.*

So are we talking about building friendships as a leadership skill or something entirely different?

Let's put this question into context using wildlife and wild places—specifically, cats. If you have a cat at home, you definitely have your own stories to add here. Typically, cats tend to be independent, choosing where they sleep and when they would like to engage with people. They might roam around the house and decide whether they want to come when they are called. They are not necessarily known for being overly cooperative and may even be described as aloof (although affectionate and loving). Basically, cats tend to do as they please, and, generally, cat owners can let them do just that.

Until, that is, you need the cats to go somewhere, like to the vet or to evacuate your home in a hurricane. Then, this aloof, do-as-you-please behavior becomes troublesome as you try to get each cat into their cat carrier. And if one of the cats is hurt or sick and therefore needs to see the vet, or the hurricane has shifted course, so you need to leave as soon as possible (and you are feeling really stressed), the tensions in your home are probably escalating, and your anxiety is most likely not helping the situation. Unless your cats are highly trained or exceptionally laid-back, they are probably not thrilled about heading into a cat carrier, so out come the claws and teeth. You are now, as the saying goes, attempting the difficult task of "herding cats."

Can anything help in this situation? Yes. And we know this well because a few months ago, Tasman, Kepler, and I were in this exact scenario: A third hurricane in less than three months was heading toward our home, and tensions were high. The first hurricane flooded our garage for four days and brought us a cat who had weathered the storm on our neighbor's back porch. This new cat arrived understandably highly anxious as well as exhausted and starving. She slept for the first few days anywhere she wanted to in the house until she became alert enough to realize two other cats already lived here. So by the time the third storm hit, the three cats had learned to coexist but not necessarily get along. And then the three humans found themselves attempting to herd the three cats into carriers.

What did we instinctively rely on? Knowing these cats as individuals. Rather than attempting the same strategy with all the animals, we immediately separated them, knowing that our oldest (seventeen-year-old) cat, Max, would be the most stressed and uncooperative. We knew the youngest, Poppy, would be slightly clueless as to what was happening, so we put her in her carrier first—success! The newest arrival, Athena, had only lived with us for a few weeks, so she was the unknown variable, but she was by far the biggest cat and therefore didn't fit in our small carriers. So we changed course, borrowed a soft-top carrier, and used only slow and calm movements as much as possible (which we theorized would not trigger any storm-related stress).

Were any of our cats overly happy with us? Nope. Did they agree with our decision to put them into cat carriers? Absolutely not. Did we make this decision because we could see the bigger picture (a hurricane heading toward our home) even though we knew the claws would come out? Yep.

But at no time did we get mad at our cats for not agreeing with our decision. We didn't start yelling (even though we were frustrated), we didn't chase them around the house, and we didn't wonder if they would love us at the end of the day. We knew that we were making the best decision we could in the moment, and we relied on our knowledge of who they were as individuals to coax them into cooperating.

When you are the leader and you can see the (metaphorical) storm approaching, it is your responsibility to make the decision about what to do. Even if everyone is not in agreement, you will have built up enough trust from your team that they will still respect you. However, getting them to act is a different story, and knowing each person as an individual will help you motivate them in the most personal way possible. You will most likely feel like you are herding cats. And although it can be painful, it is possible if you have connections with your people.

It's easy to look at a cat and just think they are cuddly and cute. Sometimes, we stop there and think we know what that cat is all about. But if you take the time to develop a strong connection and understand the animal's unique needs, then you know who that cat is as an individual. And while you'll not necessarily be friends with your cat, you will be connected.

It's easy to look at a person and just know them on the surface level. And no, I am not advising you to become friends with every person on your team, in your club, or working with you on your project. That takes time and investment on a different level with an entirely different outcome. And at a certain point, you might be leading so many people that this is not even possible, even if you wanted to become friends with everyone. But instead, what can and should be your goal is knowing enough about each person so that you "understand, are aware of, sensitive to, and vicariously experience the feelings, thoughts, and experience of another."[1]

In short, you are now nurturing one of the most crucial leadership skills: empathy.

KEPLER'S LEADERSHIP TALE

Kepler is basically an avatar. He is so deeply connected with people in his life that I'm sure if one of us were to start bleeding right now, he would as well. He can sense when I am sad before I've said a word, brings Tasman a cat for her lap when she needs one, and is as comfortable with cheers as he is with tears.

He is this way with friends, teammates, classmates, and even relative strangers as well. He may be quiet and introverted, but that does not mean he is not paying attention. In fact, I think flying under the radar screen so well actually helps him as a leader because he's spending his time reading body language and picking up on context clues rather than trying to think of what to say next in a classroom discussion or team meeting. By the time words are spoken by other people, Kepler typically has a sense of what they are going to be. And when someone needs support, he shows up next to that person—literally.

While this Leadership Tale is not outright tied to mental health, it was originally inspired by a conversation with a therapist that Kepler was seeing during his battle with depression. As I've shared Tasman's mental health journey with her permission, Kepler has also given me permission to write about his journey in hopes of normalizing conversations about mental health and its place in leadership.

As he attended therapy, he learned the difference between his struggles with the very real and overwhelming depressive episodes he was experiencing and the beautiful and powerful ability that he has to identify and relate to other people's feelings. It was crucial to me that he did not associate the two to the point that he wanted to "get rid" of his empathy (if that was even possible).

His therapist understood this delicate balance, so in an effort to encourage Kepler on his journey, she accurately summed it up in one statement: "Kepler, empathy is your superpower."

And Kepler's Leadership Tale was born.

Kepler: It's hard for me to know what to write because this is just how I am. I can sense what someone is feeling, and that helps me when I need to work with them because if someone is feeling embarrassed or frustrated, I know—no matter how much they try to hide it. Being able to figure out what people truly feel helps me figure out how to help them.

It is just not possible to be a "leader" one minute and a "person" the next; you are simultaneously both, and so are the people on your team. If you are going to show up as your whole self (see Leadership Tale #6), that includes the not-so-perfect parts too. The more you reveal your (metaphorical) scars, the more you create space for others to do so. And the more you share or at least try not to cover up the times when you don't feel mentally healthy or strong, the more you create a safe and accepting space for those around you to feel seen.

Kepler has gone on to manage his depressive episodes and does not experience them as frequently. He has also learned to celebrate and even champion the times when he can sense when someone needs support—even when he is not friends with them—because the reality is, just like in leadership, you do not have to be friends with someone to have empathy for them.

There are signs you can pay attention to before taking a chance to show up for people who might need you in the moment. The person who looks upset after they froze up during their portion of a group presentation in front of the class—what could you say to them on your way out the door? The person who missed the shot that would have been the winning score in the soccer game—can you give them a high five anyway? The person whose responsibility it was to finish their part of the project by noon on Saturday, but their car broke down, so they had to get towed and now have to find the money to fix their car—can you set aside your frustration long enough to ask how they are doing and how you can help?

This is not about absolving someone of responsibility. It is about when life happens and people need empathy instead of judgment. It's about the moments when friends are not there and someone looks lonely or outcast. It's the fact that people need champions in bad times as well as good. It's the fact that even when faced with prickly bits and sharp claws, underneath it all is a person.

If you are going to lead them, how can you know them as people first? And just watch what happens when you do. Not only will the people around you lean in more, but you will also start attracting others craving a leader who sees them as a person. And then the leaders around you will wonder what's happening. They might be curious as to how you are connecting with so many people and why you are leading in a successful and influential way. They might ask you your secret, and I hope you share.

Not only does empathy have a place in leadership, but it is also a core responsibility. And if you can claim this and make this central to how you lead? Then you have claimed empathy in its rightful place: as a leadership superpower.

Tasman: I take on many leadership roles at my school, and by far, my favorite position includes frequently conversing with underclassmen in order to successfully execute my plans for a weekly chapel service. I have absolutely no intention of becoming friends with freshmen, but they are knowledgeable about the technology I need to access for the speakers, the video screens, and the lighting. A lot of work goes into our services, and I have a wonderful team to support me. Every piece of it is timed to the minute, and we are prepared days in advance, so it is incredibly stressful if one part of the team is unable to complete their jobs. However, I understand that we are students first. If one member has a test they are really stressed about, I will do everything I can to find a temporary replacement for them so they can focus on school. Being an empathetic leader means my team will trust me enough to tell me when they need to take a step back, and they will respect me enough to come back ready to work as soon as they are capable.

LEADERSHIP IN REAL LIFE

When I am solely in the role of team member, I usually have lots of ideas about how I would do things if I were the leader. Not all of these ideas are critical, and I am typically a full-on supporter of our leader, but it's just how my brain works—I'm constantly thinking of ideas and new possibilities.

Back when I had been working at the aquarium for about four years, I was offered a promotion. I was so excited I couldn't stand it—finally! It was a chance to be in meetings with other leaders, make big-scale decisions, and take my team and department as high as we could go!

I kept a mini-tape recorder in my car (yes, this was the pre-cell-phones-that-were-really-mini-computers era) to voice record ideas as they came to me while I was driving. I kept a notepad with me at all times so I could jot down thoughts and visions. I was constantly dreaming and doing, creating our future for impact. Full steam ahead!

The most difficult part of this transition—moving from team member to leader of the team—was realizing that I was now the person in charge. When I was a team member, I freely shared my excitement and voiced frustration about the people in charge or the decisions being made. But now that I was the person in charge? Now that I was the one making the decision? Who could I share that with? I'm sure my team members felt those same moments of excitement or frustration, but I was no longer a part of the conversation.

I was getting used to this new way of being, actively filtering out what I shared so that I didn't overburden them, until one day, I had a particularly difficult encounter with some other leaders. Usually I was able to keep my frustration in check, not show it on my face, and come back to our offices ready to support my team.

But not this day. I walked back toward our team offices, looking as dejected and defeated as I felt. My feet moved slower than normal, my shoulders sagged, and I just wanted to get to my private office as quickly as possible and close the door before the tears came.

CONTINUED →

In my office, I put down my bag on my desk and turned to shut the door, and there she was: one of my team members. I hadn't heard her approach or noticed that she'd been standing behind me. Without a word, she reached out and gave me a giant hug. Then, she released me and started walking out the door, but then she suddenly stopped and turned back around.

"I know you're not going to tell me what's wrong or what happened, so I'm not even going to ask. But I also know that whatever happened in that meeting, you had the best interests of our team at heart, and we are grateful to you. You never have to tell us the details. Just know we've got your back too. And it's clear you needed a hug," she quietly explained.

It was also immediately clear how much I needed empathy in that moment. I never told my team what had happened. They never asked. But they empathized.

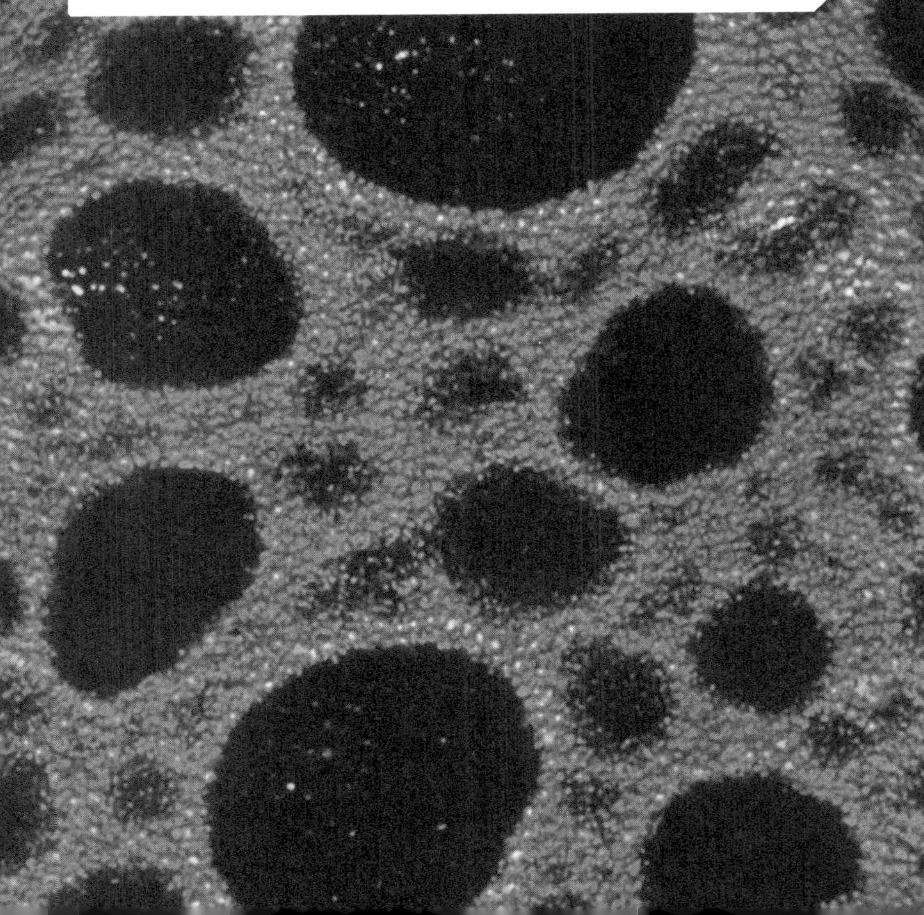

LEADERSHIP FIELD NOTES

- Ask each person you are leading one question to get to know them better. Then, pay attention to *how* they are answering the question as well as *what* they are saying.
- Check in with your teammates about how they are feeling about the upcoming game or project in addition to whether they know what will be expected of them.
- Be brave in sharing a frustration or struggle you are having so you can encourage others to do the same.

INTO THE WILD FOR A BRAIN BREAK

WITH TASMAN

Parents can be really embarrassing, especially when you're a teenager. Pretty much everything your parents do seems uncool or, at the very least, weird. I know a lot of my friends deal with this, and I'm sure you do too. So do I, but in a different way. Having a biologist for a mother is awesome until the dinner conversation resorts to just how cool it is that sea cucumbers throw up their guts as a defense mechanism (very appetizing).

My favorite "weird" thing about my mom is her obsession with birds. Her contact name in my phone is "Bird Nerd." Just this morning, she was driving to an appointment and was almost late when she missed her turn because she spotted an osprey flying above her, carrying a big fish, so she needed to follow and cheer it on. It's a unique passion for sure, but I love it. All mothers have weird obsessions: collecting snow globes, decorating for Christmas way too early, etc. My mom likes birds (and echinoderms).

LEADERSHIP TALE #6

HOW YOU SHOW UP IS HOW YOU LEAD

(WE SEE YOU, POISON DART FROGS)

"You have everything you need right now."

—KAY OYEGUN, WRITER, PRODUCER, DIRECTOR

When I first got my dream job at my favorite worldrenowned aquarium, I was ecstatic to be learning about and working alongside all of these amazingly awesome animals I had been reading about for so long: loggerhead sea turtles, nurse sharks, green moray eels, stoplight parrotfish, giant Pacific octopus, piranha, paddlefish, Pacific white-sided dolphin, beluga whales . . . frogs?

I was on a team of people who would rotate through various locations in the aquarium, and at each spot, our job was part explaining cool facts and sharing conservation action ideas about the animals we were standing next to and part answering guestservices questions about which bus to take back to their hotel or a good restaurant to eat at downtown. It was fast-paced and kept me on my toes (literally) in every sense of the word because I never knew the questions or conversations I would be having.

I had a message to share about the wildlife and wild places the aquarium was supporting, but I also was an important link to their overall experience not only in the aquarium but also in our city and beyond. I met people from all over the world, heard languages spoken I'd never heard before, and never got tired of seeing someone's eyes light up when they saw a sea otter for the first time and laughed at their underwater antics.

Each day brought the excitement of seeing new animal behaviors up close while interpreting for guests . . . until the day my schedule included a rotation into our new special exhibit called "Frogs!" I was not thrilled. The idea of standing around talking about amphibians when I could be explaining why a paddlefish swims around with its mouth wide open from time to time was, well, boring. The quicker the two-hour time slot passed, the quicker I could be back talking about stingrays and penguins.

Reluctantly, trying to muster my usual enthusiasm, I headed inside the frog exhibit—and stopped in my tracks. There wasn't the usual line of visitors slowly walking along the walls of an exhibit in a straight line, looking into tanks at their height, stopping when they were interested in an animal, and moving on.

No, the frog exhibit was a different story! The exhibit designers decided to mimic the natural habitats of the frogs, so instead of placing the tanks at eye level for a human, they chose to place the habitats where the frogs would actually be living: on the ground. In the wild, most frog species prefer to camouflage or hide near rocks or foliage so they're inherently harder to find. Therefore, they also are generally found living on ground level.

I stared in wonder, watching adults and children scrambling all over the place, crawling around and squatting down to find frogs that might be living in the corner of a tank that was at the same level as their foot. Instead of a potentially boring exhibit, the energy in the room was buzzing as the active search continued for a leg or two beady eyes that would indicate the presence of a frog.

Except in one spot.

Openly defying the design experience of the room, one exhibit stood out because barely anyone moved as they stared at the habitat. They were not whispering to each other, trying desperately to find a hint of a living creature. They were not actively seeking out a sign to tell them the animal's name, how long they live, or where they're found in the wild. Instead, everyone just stood in awe, and I even heard a squeal of childish delight—because there, in front of their eyes, were the unmistakable splashes of neon yellow, orange, and blue.

No one could possibly miss the bold stances of the poison dart frogs.

ARE YOUR COLORS BOLD ENOUGH TO STAND OUT AS A LEADER?

When you walk into a room, how do you know who the leader is?

Sometimes, the context clues are obvious: The leader is the person sitting behind the desk or standing in front of the active board with a slide presentation already pulled up.

Sometimes, it's less obvious, and you have to glance around a bit before you notice a person standing at the other door shaking people's hands as they walk in, asking their names, and inviting them to take a seat wherever they would like.

Maybe you start reading everyone's name tags, looking for a job title you might recognize. Maybe you ask the person next to you if they know who's the one in charge.

But what about the times when none of these clues exist—when you walk into a room and everyone is milling about? Maybe they're helping themselves to juice and donuts in one corner or standing around in small groups because they're not sure yet where to sit.

Imagine for a moment that you are standing next to me at the Frogs! exhibit at my favorite aquarium. We've looked at all the other habitats and actively searched for hiding amphibians, and now we've come to the exhibit with poison dart frogs. No more searching, no more asking each other if one of us has found the animal yet—just the two of us staring with open mouths at the brightly colored creatures hanging out in the mud or on a green leaf. Do we even need to wonder what we're supposed to be looking for? Nope. The animal is sitting right in front of us. And it really doesn't matter right away which species of poison dart frogs we're observing; we're content to watch them watch us before they hop on their way to a different part of their habitat. They seem to command our attention just by sitting still in all their brightly colored glory.

Of course, they're highly toxic, so they don't need to camouflage themselves like other frog species.[1] Their brightly colored skin warns predators that they are not suitable prey. If an unaware predator attempts a meal, the toxin on their skin can paralyze or even kill the predator. In fact, one of the deadliest species, the golden poison frog, has enough poison to kill ten people![2] Most birds, fish, and snakes that might normally go after a frog would be wise to avoid this one.

So all the poison dart frogs sit out in the open, unconcerned about any predators that could be close by. They don't vocally announce their presence, engage in behavior that might indicate they're poisonous, or in any other way shout from the rooftops that they are there. They simply are. You might feel like you can even sense their presence.

Now, come back into the room I asked you to walk into earlier, and take another look around. Is there anyone who is walking a little straighter, head held high? Or someone who looks people in the eye with confidence and is clearly moving between groups to meet people they don't know? Is there someone who seems (literally) so comfortable in their own skin that they don't rely on introducing themselves with their job title, their last name, or degree, and have even seemed to have (intentionally) forgotten their name tag—they just introduce themselves with their first name? Or someone who speaks quietly and is intently engaged in conversation with one person at a time, clearly focused on making sure to listen effectively to what the person is saying before they move on to the next conversation?

The most impactful and influential leaders I know, teach, and coach are the ones who do not have to *tell* people they are the leader. They simply *act* as the leader they are. When they are in a room, they are the ones who carry themselves with confidence, whether they are gregariously interacting with everyone in the room at once or quietly engaging with one person at a time. They are the ones who are on time, pay attention, actively participate, and remember people's names. And even if they are not the person in charge of that particular meeting or event, they are still leading through their supportive behavior and by being a team player.

In short, they are like the poison dart frogs in the room. They show up ready to lead, unconcerned with announcing they are there because they just are, and act accordingly. They don't have to tell people they are the leader; they just lead.

This is all part of a concept called *executive* or *leadership presence*.

But really, what it's about is less talking and more doing. It is showing up in the way you want to lead and then just leading.

YOU HAVE SEVEN SECONDS

Every opportunity is a leadership opportunity. Every time you are on the field, in the studio, in the auditorium, or in the lab, you have a choice of how you show up. And that choice directly affects your influence and impact as a leader. And if it's the first time people are meeting you, you get one shot at a first impression. It's commonly believed that people will have a solid impression of who you are in the first—

Seven seconds.[3]

Pause here, and count down: 7, 6, 5, 4, 3, 2, 1 . . .

Time's up.

That's it. The person you are talking to and the people around you have formed an opinion about you. And you have created your own opinion about them. Whether it is "right" or not is not entirely within your control either. What *is* in your control is the way in which you showed up—and this is directly related to the words you brainstormed in Leadership Tale #1, in which you decided what it truly meant for you to be a great leader.

Just as you chose the words that describe who you want to be as a leader, you can also choose how you want to show up as a leader. To make this more practical, think about these four leadership presence buckets:

DIAGRAM 4: LEADERSHIP PRESENCE BUCKETS

1. **Mentally:** What is your mindset? If you are nervous and don't feel like you belong, the people around you will sense that. If you have taken the time to prepare, are confident in your skills, and plan to regroup if (when) you fail, then you are ready to engage as a leader.
2. **Physically:** How are you presenting yourself in alignment with who you are as a leader and your responsibilities? This is a delicate balance between authenticity and appropriateness for the group and setting. If you're not a suit-wearing kind of person, seriously consider whether this is necessary: Following a dress code is one thing; wearing something because you think someone won't take you seriously in anything else is another. Aim to present yourself in a professional yet personal manner. Depending on the setting, this may mean clean clothes and comfortable shoes, or other times, it means steel-toe boots and safety goggles. And once you arrive, be intentional, stand confidently, and own your space as a leader.

3. **Emotionally:** Are you ready emotionally to connect—to flex your empathetic muscle as necessary? Showing up and being present as the leader means going all in with the emotions present as well; these could range from extreme excitement and celebration to high levels of concern and downright frustration. You may see these emotions displayed on faces, hear them exclaimed in the room, and feel them yourself. Staying in the moment through a range of emotions helps you better engage and build trust as a leader, and it shows your deep respect for everyone present.
4. **Energetically:** If you've thoroughly ramped up your energy on your resilience bell curve, then you are ready to show up as the leader. Be cognizant of when you need to step away, when you need to lean in more, and when you need to simply take a breath before moving on to the next task or conversation. If you feed off the energy in the room, be conscious of giving back to others who need it. If energy tends to drain out of you when surrounded by people, honor this part of you by taking time for yourself as needed. Then, give respect to the back end of your resilience bell curve to rest and recharge so you can show up fully as the leader the next time.

I've specifically grouped these leadership presence concepts into "buckets" because, depending on the situation you are going into, you may need to fill up one bucket more than another. Maybe, on a particular day, you feel mentally ready to show up because you're excited about the program you've been working on, but you woke up sick, so energetically, you're run down. For that day, you'll need to focus more intently on your energy so you can still show up as fully as possible as the leader. Be gentle with yourself as you figure out where you need to focus your attention, but be aware that all four of these buckets are important in leadership presence. You cannot leave one behind and think no one will notice. You need all four of these buckets to show up how you want to lead.

BE MORE THAN A NAME TAG LEADER

Acting as a leader and having the word "leader" somewhere in (or associated with) your title for your job or role is not the same thing. It never will be. Every opportunity you waste when you could have stepped up to lead but you were waiting for someone to give you the title of leader is an opportunity you will never get back. And every moment you need to introduce yourself as the leader before you act, relying on the title listed on your name tag to add gravitas, is a moment you erode part of your credibility as the leader and reduce your impact.

People, projects, programs, and possibilities do not wait around for someone to tell them they are the leader. They unite behind people who simply lead.

I have a collection of name tags from all the titles I've held over the years. Looking at these name tags brings back fond memories not just of the zoos, aquariums, amusement parks, YMCA camps, restaurants, bookstores, and more at which I have worked, but more importantly, of the people I worked alongside, the people I led, the people I met as guests and customers, and the communities, wildlife, and wild places we worked so hard to positively impact. Someday, these name tags will get broken or lost, but the stories will remain. My titles have changed over the years, but my heart for leaders and passion for wildlife and wild places have not.

Whether I meet you as Julie or as Ms. Henry with a bunch of letters, degrees, and associated organizations I've worked at after my name, I'm the same person. I don't need anyone, any place, or any title to validate or reinforce my work as a leader. I don't even need the word "leader" anywhere around my name. I'm just as comfortable stepping up when I need to as I am supporting as others lead. I've got plenty of ideas I will still work to bring to life and programs I plan to lead.

So if we ever get a chance to meet in person, I will introduce myself as Julie and want to meet you as you. I will see you as far more than what any name tag could ever pretend to bestow on you. I am cheering you on as you show up and stand tall in every situation going forward in which you can show up as the leader you are—without waiting for a (or the next) title, without waiting for someone to go first, without waiting to feel completely ready.

Leave the name tag at home. Show up as you.

That will always be enough.

Tasman: It's really hard to tell who the leader is when you're at the circus. Equipment is constantly being rigged, the flying trapeze is moving, and people are everywhere. It's easy to get confused or get the dynamic mixed up.

If you look hard enough, in the back corner of my arena, you will most likely see a short red-haired woman sitting in a chair and writing in a little notebook. What you can't see is that she is a member of one of the most illustrious circus families dating back to 1840. She has performed all over the world, from events in Las Vegas and cruise lines to her work as the first-ever Tinkerbell to fly out of Cinderella's Castle at Walt Disney World. You wouldn't know this just by seeing her or even by speaking to her because these are not the most important things she has to offer.

Mara is always choreographing the next routine for her students. She is always prepared months before every other act, and performers tend to respect her authority even without knowledge of her successes. I have been lucky enough to participate in her acts for several years now, and I continue to recognize the impact she has on all of us—especially without the name tag.

Kepler: I was training at the circus, and all of a sudden, everyone stopped and was looking up at the flying trapeze net. Of course, I looked up too and saw someone I didn't know. I had never seen him before, but just by how high he was swinging and how precise his movements were, I knew he was someone important. I later found out that he is currently the #1 trapeze artist in the world, but I could already tell that he was a very confident and skilled artist by the way he carried himself. I never talked to him directly; I just knew because of how he was.

LEADERSHIP IN REAL LIFE

I've celebrated many colleagues over the years as they have earned more responsibility, new jobs, bigger titles, and highly sought-after roles of all sorts. Some have hit the ground running—ready to jump in, get to know their team members, and start making the impact they've always dreamed of having. They go all in and start leading.

And some do not.

Success is not always immediate. The measures of success can certainly be different depending on leadership positions, the situation someone is walking into, the person's familiarity with the company, etc. But what do I see most often as the #1 reason leaders do not flourish as soon as possible in their new roles?

Their name tags. And their desire to make sure people know what the title on their new name tag says.

I get it; it's exciting, they've worked so hard, they're proud, and they want to share that now they're the leader. This does not always come from a negative place. Sometimes the leader doesn't even know they're doing it. But the following conversation is often what happens.

Me to the leader: "How's it going? How are you settling into your new role? What are you most excited about?"

Leader: "It's going *fantastic*! I think everyone is really excited to have me here! I'm so happy to have this new role! I'm going to make such a difference! I've been able to get onto so many new committees and meet so many new people, and I have a really exciting future ahead of me!"

Me to the team: "How's it going? How is the new leader settling in? What are you most excited about?"

Team: "Well, we're really excited to have them here. They have a great track record and bring a wonderful new perspective. But they have spent so much time and effort talking about how excited they are to be the leader that they haven't really taken the time yet to get to know us, our challenges, and the possibilities ahead. We're starting to get frustrated, thinking that maybe our leader is more excited about people knowing they're the leader instead of actually leading."

Trust me; I've seen it many, many times: people who go to all the trouble of earning a title they've always wanted, then they keep talking about it as if they're trying to still prove they deserve it. The more they talk, the less they do. And they somehow forget the old adage that "actions speak louder than words."

Or maybe in this context, "actions speak louder than name tags."

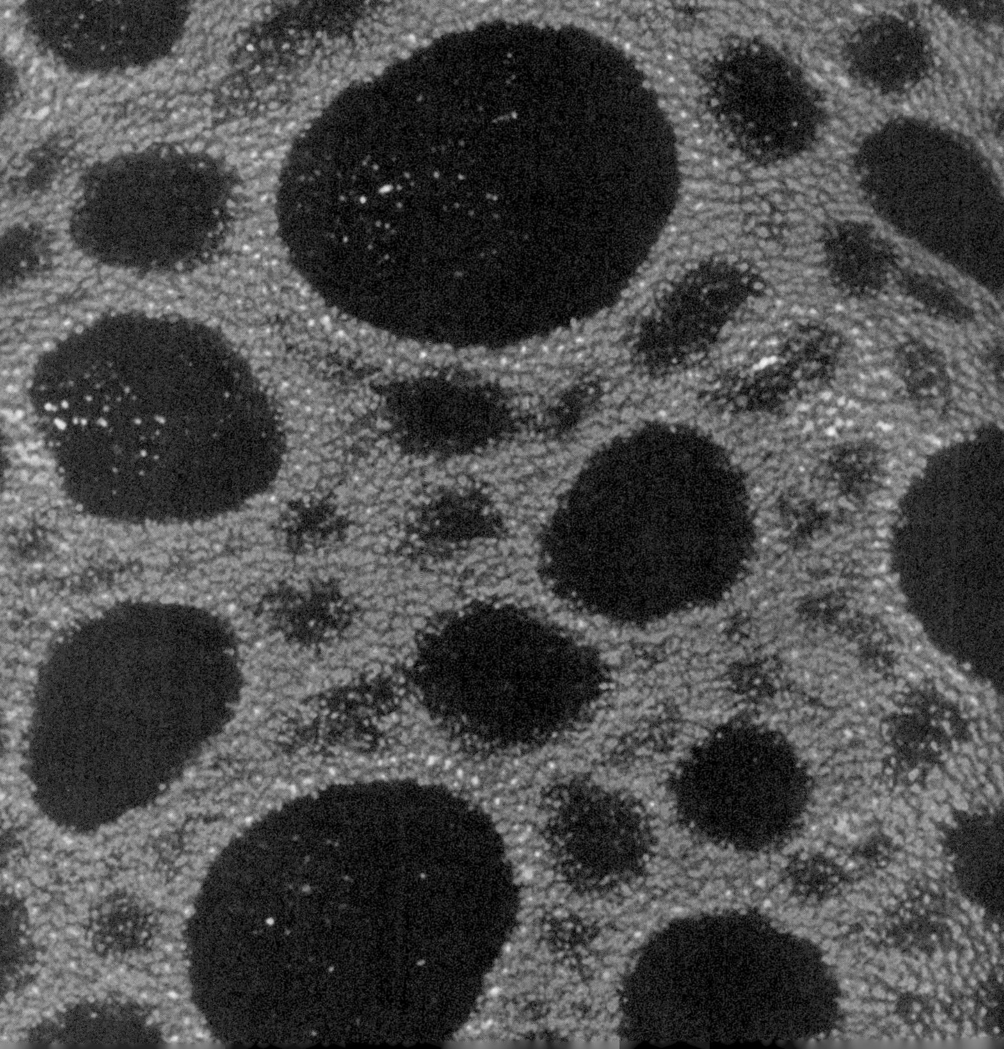

LEADERSHIP FIELD NOTES

- Start to pay attention to how different leaders assert their "leadershipness" in various scenarios (without announcing they are the leader), and choose actions you want to try for yourself.
- Choose one of the four leadership presence buckets that is challenging for you, and think about a time in the near future (ideally the next month or so) when you will have an opportunity to show up as a leader. Write down two ideas from that bucket about how you can proactively decide to show up as the leader you want to be.
- Lean into the truth that every opportunity is a leadership opportunity, and resolve to never waste one again. This is not about perfection; this is about intention.

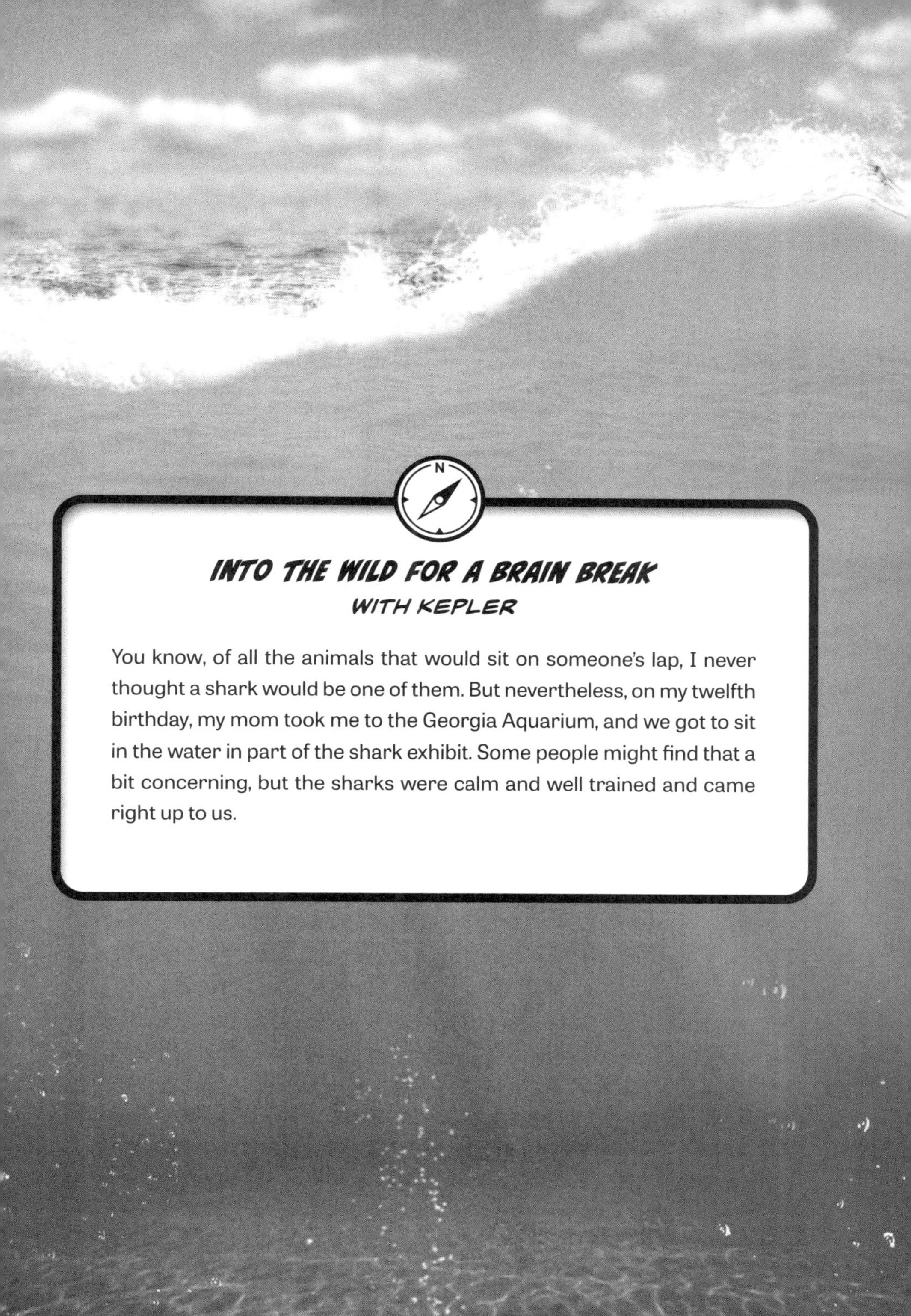

INTO THE WILD FOR A BRAIN BREAK

WITH KEPLER

You know, of all the animals that would sit on someone's lap, I never thought a shark would be one of them. But nevertheless, on my twelfth birthday, my mom took me to the Georgia Aquarium, and we got to sit in the water in part of the shark exhibit. Some people might find that a bit concerning, but the sharks were calm and well trained and came right up to us.

LEADERSHIP FIELD GUIDE: HOW IT'S GOING

"It's no use going back to yesterday, because I was a different person then."

—LEWIS CARROLL, ALICE'S ADVENTURES IN WONDERLAND

Time to check in and see how it's going! We've covered a lot of ground (or maybe dived deep into the sea), and we want to give you a chance to reflect. Ideas are only helpful if they are put into action, so here's your chance to see where you started as a leader in comparison with how it's going now so that you can chart your way forward with intention.

LEADERSHIP FIELD GUIDE REFLECTION #1: WHO AM I AS A LEADER?

Before you look back at your thoughts in the "Leadership Field Guide: How It Started," write down three words that immediately come to mind when asked to complete this prompt:

TODAY'S DATE: ________________

As a leader, I am:

____

____

____

Now, turn back to the first field guide (page 24). If your words are the same, do you have a new perspective on them? If your words are different, why did you choose a new word now?

The important piece of this reflection is not whether your words changed. It is perfectly acceptable if you still identify with and own the words you chose at the beginning of the book—just as much as it is perfectly fine if you now have three completely different words. Everyone's journey is unique. What's important here is that you *intentionally choose* and *champion* your words. I want you to get so excited about them that you would shout them from the rooftop if asked! They are who you are and choose to be as a leader.

LEADERSHIP FIELD GUIDE REFLECTION #2: WHAT DO I THINK LEADERSHIP IS ALL ABOUT?

Go back to the drawing you created in the first leadership field guide (page 26), and use these questions to reflect:

TODAY'S DATE: ________________

1. Does this drawing still capture what you think about when you picture a "leader doing leadership"? Why or why not?
2. Which of the six Leadership Tales do you either already see

reflected in your drawing or would you incorporate if you drew a picture now?

3. If you drew yourself as the leader, why did you choose to do so? If you drew someone else, what did you capture about their leadership?
4. What additional component(s) would you like to add to your picture now—a demonstration of empathy? Showing up more as yourself as a leader? Other?

For this reflection, I want you to consider the unspoken parts of leadership that can be better represented through drawing than through words. We can *say* we want to be a certain type of leader, but it is when we *act* that those leadership qualities truly come to life. Drawing leadership allows you to capture leadership in action.

FUTURE LEADERSHIP FIELD GUIDES

The framework provided by these companion leadership field guides is one that you can use throughout your leadership journey. The simple, straightforward prompts can anchor your leadership growth and provide an accurate measure of progress. You can even use these prompts with people you lead now and in the future.

Remember where we started together: with ideas.

Now, we are putting those ideas into action!

OVER TO YOU, LEADER

"Kites rise high against the wind, not with it."

—WINSTON CHURCHILL, PRIME MINISTER OF THE UNITED KINGDOM

When I was a freshman in college, I wanted desperately to join a particular student-driven organization that targeted professional development and leadership skills. It was a very sought-after club, so they had an application and interview process. I was nervous to even try to get in, but my excitement, interest, and motivation from my friends won out, and I applied. Much to my surprise, I passed the first round and was notified that I had been granted an interview.

The day of the interview, I was a bundle of nerves. Somehow, I made my way to the right place on campus, waited (rather terrified) for my turn, and then walked into the interview room. Two upperclassmen sat on the opposite side of a long table, and the interview soon began. Everything was clipping along and I was feeling confident until they asked me, "So, Julie, what do you consider are three of your strengths and three of your weaknesses as a leader?"

I was stunned into silence.

I had never been asked that question before, and now I was faced with an insurmountable challenge. What could I say was a strength without seeming too egotistical? What did I even consider a strength of mine in the first place? And a weakness?! Should I be honest and share what I struggle with or choose one that seems more in line with what a leader should be dealing with? Were there right answers to these questions based on the type of people they were looking to let into the club? How in the world was I supposed to prep for this question? And what was I going to say now that the time had clearly gone on way too long and they were staring at me, waiting for me to say something . . . ?

So I said nothing—for a very long time—until the upperclassmen clearly felt bad for me, so they tried to help me think of some things to say. They offered some ideas that might fit me until I mumbled under my breath, "Yeah, I guess."

I did not get into the club.

Fast-forward five years, and I was a young professional working at my first career job out of college at that same world-renowned aquarium. It was literally my dream job, and every day of work felt like a fantasy come true. I would go out of my way to learn new things, stay late, come early, and offer to be a part of every project. Slowly, I was afforded opportunities to grow in responsibility, manage people as well as projects, and make tough decisions. It was as exciting as it was challenging, but I would not have had it any other way.

Then, one day, an extremely serious situation occurred that involved the health of one of my teammates and several of the people we were responsible for. Everything we had been striving for and the mission-driven focus of our day-to-day work suddenly were thrown into alignment alongside the stark reality of a life-or-death situation.

I was now faced with a complete shift in focus and attention. Not only did I need to work through my emotional reaction, but I also needed to do so relatively quickly so that I could lead those around me. I needed to find words to explain truths without stoking unnecessary fear, I had to be honest yet keep building trust, and I had to have extremely difficult conversations with people's families I had never met in person. And when, inevitably, people started freaking out, emotions were accelerating, and we were on the brink of chaos, I channeled an opposite reaction.

Surrounded by turmoil, I chose to become calm. I heard my voice decrease in volume as those around me were riddled with anxiety and high-pitched. I watched my fingers slowly pick up the phone time and time again to keep moving forward with what I needed to do.

I was twenty-three years old.

A few weeks later, my boss came to me and told me how impressed she had been with how I'd handled the situation. She complimented my ability to dial it in, stay focused, and maintain compassion and empathy while also being as straightforward and pragmatic as possible. She particularly called out my intentional calm. And while I deeply appreciated the conversation and recognition, I felt surprised. It had never occurred to me *not* to be that way; I felt like I had gone into autopilot and handled it as best I could given the examples I had seen over the years, the training I had received, and the people who supported me. Even though I had never been faced with something so difficult before and it was a complete unknown, I just went in headfirst and figured being calm was a better reaction than surrendering to my innate fear. That's what she had noticed, and that's what she was calling forth now.

Hmmmmm . . . maybe I *did* have a strength as a leader that I could have reported to the upperclassmen in the interview! I didn't know it when I was eighteen years old, but I sure discovered it when I was twenty-three. And it has continued to serve me well as a leader, because I'd like to tell you that was the last time I had to face a life-or-death situation I had to lead people through, but, of course, that's not how life goes, so you move forward as best you can. Even if you can't fully articulate what those leadership skills are yet, you have them.

Everything you have read in this book has been designed to help you think critically and choose who you want to be as a leader, building first on the unique foundation of *you*. Leading now—today—in the way you were born to lead is the best thing you can do, not only for yourself but also for the people around you and the impact and influence you want to have.

But honestly? I really hope that by this point in the book, you have more questions than answers. I hope there's been a spark lit in you that motivates you to seek out more about leadership. Maybe you're intrigued about how you can grow as a leader in your local community, which will require you to lead people of all ages. Maybe you're excited about going someplace else in the world, which will require you to learn a new language, local customs, an entirely new community of people, and how you can be effective as a leader. Maybe you're just ready to sit outside in a hammock for a bit, pondering all of the ideas we've brought forth in this book. And maybe you're furiously journaling all of the questions you have . . .

What do all of these scenarios have in common? Curiosity.

The dictionary defines curiosity as a "strong desire to know or learn something."[1] In real life, curiosity shows up when you wonder about something and ask questions.

Remember where we started together? By jumping over the side of a boat into the ocean to search for giant squid. We started by asking questions about an animal that has only recently been seen alive in its natural habitat and the ocean that is so vast we have yet to explore 95% of it. For sure, the ocean has far more unknowns in it than knowns that are just waiting to be explored and discovered.

Now, bringing this full circle, if you've ever wandered through an aquarium and seen a pink-hued creature underwater staring back at you that looks mysteriously like a Muppet, I bet you had some questions about it. Or maybe you've been playing Minecraft on your computer, and you notice an animal hanging out in an underwater cave with what seems to be electrified pieces of hair sticking out of its head. In both cases, this animal may not appear to be real, but it is. You've encountered an axolotl.

MAMA JULIE, THE MUPPETS, AND AN AXOLOTL

As you stare into the habitat at the aquarium or look more closely at the animal in the cave in your Minecraft game, you probably notice a few things: webbed feet, a long tail, and those electrified hair-like pieces sticking out of its head that actually look more like feathers with their wispy edges. If you think about animals you know that live underwater that look similar, frogs and salamanders might come to mind. And you would be correct: These animals are amphibians, which means they typically spend their early years underwater and then eventually go through metamorphosis and develop adaptations so they can live on land. As juveniles, most amphibians have webbed feet, long tails, and gills so they can breathe underwater. As they get older, their feet and tails adapt to living on land, and their gills are replaced by lungs. But there are more than 8,000 species of amphibians found throughout the world, and they don't all follow these rules.[2] One of the species that doesn't? Axolotls.

Axolotls are amphibians—specifically, a type of salamander—that don't go through metamorphosis. That means the axolotls you are looking at in the aquarium or in your game could be young or old; you'd never know their age by looking at them like you would a type of salamander that went through a juvenile phase of living underwater and then an adult phase of living on land. Axolotls live their whole lives underwater, looking like juveniles (even though they get bigger). So basically . . .

Axolotls are animals that never grow up. They stay "childlike" forever.

That face that looks like a Muppet? It always makes me smile—almost as much as the real Muppets do. No matter how old I get, I will always love the Muppets. And axolotls will always have that Muppet face.

Right now, you are in a stage of development as a leader. And you will keep growing, changing, and evolving throughout your life. But one of the qualities I want to both encourage and challenge you not to lose is that of curiosity.

When we are young, we ask questions about everything. It was my favorite part of being a parent to Kepler and Tasman when they were very young: listening to them wonder about everything around them. They asked questions I never would have even thought to ask and plenty of questions to which I had no idea what the answers even were.

As they have gotten older, we've worked hard together to create a space and environment for questions to still be asked. Sometimes, we get worried that our questions will be seen as stupid or that we should already know the answer. Sometimes, we hold back because we're afraid what others will think about us, and that can lead us to stifling questions before they even arise.

So as we close out our book and our time together, I want to take off my author hat and put on my Mama Julie hat. As a young child, you had many questions and wondered about the world around you. As a young leader, you have just as many questions and wonder about direction and actions to take. This sense of curiosity about leadership is not only exactly what you should be feeling right now, but it's also the sense I hope you always retain.

I encourage you to be the axolotls of leadership.

I challenge you to be the leaders who never grow up and lose your curiosity.

Your lived experiences, roles, and responsibilities will change, and you will have even more wisdom to bring to each scenario. But underneath it all, you can still be a Muppet-faced, axolotl-like leader ready and willing to ask a question. I promise you this will serve you and the people you lead well.

How? I don't know; that remains to be seen. That is the magic of curiosity. It's about questions, not answers.

What I do know? We need more axolotls in the world of leadership.

We need you.

FROM US AS YOUTH TO YOU

THE FINAL WORD

"Every individual matters. Every individual has a role to play. Every individual makes a difference."

—DR. JANE GOODALL, PRIMATOLOGIST AND ANTHROPOLOGIST

Even if nobody actually talks to you about leadership and you don't see many things you do as "being a leader," all of us can lead in our own way. I can't really relate to my mom and my sister in how they love to talk in front of big groups of people they don't know, but I can still motivate people and accomplish goals in different ways. If you're like me and don't really like to give speeches or be an outgoing and loud leader, just know that the introverted leader is just as essential as the extroverted one.

—Kepler

I hope you understand that the analogies and lessons we used in this book do not end here. These are things we constantly live out and teach in every aspect of our lives. My mom always says to me, "Give yourself the best chance," which is resilience, and "Mi casa, su casa," which is empathy. "Lead in the way you were born to lead" is the myth of greatness. "Finish strong" is about presence. I am so blessed to have been raised by someone who teaches me these lessons any chance she gets. And I'm even luckier to see my mom live these lessons. People often compare me to my mother, and I think that the most similar trait we have is our method of leadership. We hold ourselves the same way: We treat people with kindness, and we always show up with a smile. This is who we are. Leaders are all different, just as humans are all different. I hope that we will one day live in a world where people recognize this as the blessing it is. The world needs unique leaders. The world needs you.

—Tasman

ACKNOWLEDGMENTS

FROM JULIE

Some people pick up a book and immediately read the last page, the endorsements, or maybe even the "About the Author" section to decide whether they want to invest their time and money. For me, I always go right to the "Acknowledgments" because I want to understand more about the people who make the author who they are and, as a result, the story or message they are driven to share.

For this book, my gratitude is grounded first in my admiration for the teachers and mentors without whom I would not be the leader (or person) I am today but also without whom this book would quite literally not exist. To Mr. Uhl—my high school AP biology teacher who gave me my first shark to dissect, which solidified my love of zoology. To Dr. Ann Haley MacKenzie and Dr. Kaufman—my two college professors who collectively understood that my passion fell somewhere in the intersection of doing science, teaching leadership, and inspiring people about the natural world and helped me carve my path with all its unknown bits. To Penny Jarrett—my intern coordinator at Cincinnati Zoo and Botanical Garden, who had a never-ending-stream-of-consciousness "let's go explore this today at the zoo!" which led to behind-the-scenes adventures like unloading bags and bags of ice into an exhibit in the newly constructed bird house (among other memorable encounters) that I will cherish forever.

To the incomparable Greenleaf Book Group team who had my back through three hurricanes, two deaths that rocked my world, and the normal life events that come with writing a book—I am grateful for all of you, especially Erin Brown, Morgan Robinson, Scott James, Justin Branch, Jen Glynn, Brian Phillips, Neil Gonzalez, Jeanette Smith, and Meilee Bridges. To my dear friends and colleagues for fact-checking and for their unwavering belief in both me and this message, especially Nette Pletcher, Jim Wharton, Bill Street, Terry O'Connor, Nancy Hotchkiss, Debbi Stone, Sean Russell, Rachel Bergren, and Susan Hedgcock. To Kevin Stone and Olivia Stone—the amazing father–daughter team who brought these Tales to life through creative illustrations. To Michaela Ristaino for capturing photos of us in our natural habitat at Mote Aquarium. To the people in my life who show up, have my back, and walk alongside me. To my family for being the best cheerleaders and unofficial marketing team helping to shout from the rooftops about this book. To Sarah Rivera for the endless supply of creativity, support, and belief in youth as leaders now. And to my Street Team—how much fun it was to launch this book with you!

To Tasman and Kepler—this book is what it is because of you. Thank you for trusting me, having fun, and sharing your vulnerabilities as well as your passions in service of others. I will forever treasure the journey of writing this book together. I love you from the bottom of the Tasman Sea to the Kepler Satellite and back!

And lastly, to Dr. Brian Davis, the late president and CEO of Georgia Aquarium. No matter how far you climbed up the leadership ladder and how many degrees you earned, boards you served on, teams you managed, barriers you shattered, or projects you championed, it was always about the people you could impact—more specifically, the youth. Whether speaking to a room of thousands or one-on-one, you were always intently focused on making each person feel seen and heard, and you sought ways to raise them up. I can't remember a time in my professional life when I did not know you, but I do know that those twenty-five years were not enough. And every time I start to question whether I can really do something or feel like I might be settling for less than I deserve, I know exactly what you would say to me (or I just replay the voice message I still have from you on my phone). You were the very definition of a leader who left the name tag at home and showed up as you—every time. Rest In Power, my friend, and trust that we are doing our best to continue your good work.

FROM TASMAN

Besides scuba diving to a shipwreck, writing a book is probably one of the coolest things I've ever done. I am so grateful for my mother's passion for leadership and her relentless pursuit of youth involvement. She helped me become the leader that I am today, so thank you, Mom.

I want to thank my dad for contributing 50% of my nerd genes. I have really enjoyed adding scientific input to this book (the equilibrium thing was so cool!).

Thank you to Mrs. Otto for leading me in my absolute favorite subject in all of high school and for helping me better understand my passion for science and math.

Thank you to Dr. Hedgcock, who, although not a science fan, always supported my ambitions and worked tirelessly to make me the best writer possible. I am forever grateful for your difficult yet rewarding classes.

Thank you to Mrs. White and Mr. Tedder for encouraging me to never hold back from what I am capable of. Whether that be in an academic or a spiritual setting, I am blessed to have you both as teachers.

Thank you, Mara, Tino, and Willy, for being the most incredible coaches I could ever ask for. My dedication and work ethic radically changed after joining your acts in the circus, and I miss you very much!

Thank you to my cats, who are the best moral support ever.

And last, but certainly not least, thank you to coffee.

Good luck, leaders!

FROM KEPLER

To Mrs. Agate for being the best art teacher and encouraging aspiring art students like me.

To Dr. Hedgcock for her advice, always being there for me, and understanding that I am the absent-minded professor.

To Karen for coaching me throughout all my circus years and helping me become the clown I am today.

To Robin for being my best clown buddy (as well as a great coach).

To Willy for coaching me in my only intense act so far in circus and letting me fly off backwards.

To Siena for teaching me how to ride half a bike and encouraging my showmanship skills.

To the cats for being cats.

NOTES

READY, LEADER? LET'S DIVE IN

1. Paula Palomo, "How Deep Can Open Water Divers vs. Advanced Open Water Divers Go?" Professional Association of Diving Instructors, March 1, 2023, https://blog.padi.com/how-deep-can-open-water-vs-advanced-divers-go
2. "How Deep Is the Ocean?" National Ocean Service, June 16, 2024, https://oceanservice.noaa.gov/facts/oceandepth.html
3. "Most of Our Ocean Is Unexplored," National Ocean Service, https://oceanexplorer.noaa.gov/world-oceans-day/reason-1.html
4. "Giant Squid vs. Sperm Whale," Smithsonian Ocean, January 2010, https://ocean.si.edu/ocean-life/marine-mammals/giant-squid-vs-sperm-whale
5. Clyde Roper, "Giant Squid: *Architeuthis dux*," Smithsonian Ocean, April 2018, https://ocean.si.edu/ocean-life/invertebrates/giant-squid
6. Katie Valentine, "NOAA-Funded Expedition Captures Rare Footage of Giant Squid in the Gulf of Mexico," NOAA Research, July 3, 2020, https://research.noaa.gov/noaa-funded-expedition-captures-rare-footage-of-giant-squid-in-the-gulf-of-mexico

LEADERSHIP TALE #1

1. "Vampire Bat Colony Care," North Carolina Zoo and Botanical Gardens, June 22, 2020, https://www.nczoo.org/blog/vampire-bat-colony-care
2. Paul Hormick, "Bat Pups," Bat Conservation International, July 3, 2024, https://www.batcon.org/pupping-season/
3. "Bats 101," Bat Conservation International, https://www.batcon.org/about-bats/bats-101
4. Alexander Lee, "Bats: Out of Hell?" *History Today* vol. 70, issue 10, October 2020, https://www.historytoday.com/archive/natural-histories/bats-out-hell
5. Marc Lallanilla and Callum McKelvie, "Vlad the Impaler: The Real Dracula," Live Science, December 15, 2021, https://www.livescience.com/40843-real-dracula-vlad-the-impaler.html
6. Phoebe Codling, "Why Are Bats Associated with Vampires? A Peek into the Realm of These Misunderstood Mammals This Halloween," The Great Projects, October 27, 2017, https://www.thegreatprojects.com/blog/bats-associated-with-vampires
7. "Was Dracula a Real Person?" History.com, August 3, 2023, https://www.history.com/news/was-dracula-a-real-person
8. "What Is the Largest Sea Turtle?" NOAA, https://oceanservice.noaa.gov/facts/leatherback.html

LEADERSHIP TALE #2

1. "We Know Sharks," Shark Research Institute, https://www.sharks.org/species
2. Jodie Moore, "Creature Feature: Megamouth Shark," Shark Trust, April 3, 2023, https://www.sharktrust.org/blog/creature-feature-megamouth-shark
3. The Ocean Portal Team, David Shiffman, reviewer, "Sharks:

Euselachii," Smithsonian National Museum of Natural History, August 2014, https://ocean.si.edu/ocean-life/sharks-rays/sharks

LEADERSHIP TALE #4

1. "Rocky Mountain Bighorn Sheep: *Ovis canadensis*," Denver Zoon Conservation Alliance, https://denverzoo.org/animals/rocky-mountain-bighorn-sheep

LEADERSHIP TALE #5

1. *Merriam-Webster Dictionary*, "Empathy," https://www.merriam-webster.com/dictionary/empathy

LEADERSHIP TALE #6

1. Amy Maxmen, "How Do Tropical Frogs Get Their Stunning Colors?" *Smithsonian Magazine*, August 31, 2013, https://www.smithsonianmag.com/science-nature/how-do-tropical-frogs-get-their-stunning-colors-712275
2. Sarah Graham, "Researchers Pinpoint Source of Poison Frogs' Deadly Defenses," *Scientific American*, August 9, 2005, https://www.scientificamerican.com/article/researchers-pinpoint-sour
3. "First Impressions," *Psychology Today*, https://www.psychologytoday.com/us/basics/first-impressions

OVER TO YOU, LEADER

1. *Oxford Advanced Learner's Dictionary*, "Curiosity," https://www.oxfordlearnersdictionaries.com/us/definition/english/curiosity
2. "The Importance of Amphibians," Amphibian Ark, https://www.amphibianark.org/the-crisis/the-importance-of-amphibians/

ABOUT THE AUTHORS

JULIE C. HENRY is driven to lift leaders up across industries and across generations so they can more fully lead in the way they were born to lead. She channels her experience as a senior leader in zoos and aquariums—along with decades as a keynote speaker, facilitator, consultant, and leadership coach in more than forty different industries—into teachings that are as relevant and practical as they are memorable and fun. As host of the *Leadership Tales with Tails*™ podcast along with her co-hosts Tasman and Kepler, she facilitates unedited, unfiltered conversations about leadership with guests in the field, in the studio, or anywhere in between, that are always wild.

Julie kicked off her career at Chicago's John G. Shedd Aquarium and Cincinnati Zoo and Botanical Garden and then became a senior leader at Mote Marine Laboratory and Aquarium and Busch Gardens Tampa Bay. She holds an MA in communication from the University of South Florida, an executive program certificate in sustainable business leadership from Green Mountain College, and a postgraduate diploma in outdoor education from the University of Otago, earned as a Rotary Ambassadorial Scholar to New Zealand. She earned undergraduate degrees in zoology and education from Miami University of Ohio. Julie was selected as a Toyota TogetherGreen Fellow of the National Audubon Society and chosen to participate in the Disney's Animal Kingdom/World Wildlife Fund Biodiversity Leadership Institute.

At her core, Julie is a kid from Chicago who grew up dreaming of the sea. That led her to adventures around the world, eventually calling Sarasota, Florida, home with her two teenagers, Tasman and Kepler. With a heart for leaders and a passion for wildlife and wild places, she is fired up to continue shaking up leadership stereotypes and fully champion each person's unique impact and influence on the world.

TASMAN HENRY is eighteen years old and a freshman at Florida Gulf Coast University (FGCU). She loves science—specifically physics and chemistry—and took advantage of every leadership growth opportunity she could in high school, including as a National Honor Society committee leader, executive student body chaplain, and Blazer Café chair of marketing. She is a 2025 graduate of the elite Red Troupe of the Sailor Circus Academy in Sarasota, Florida, where she performed as an aerialist on the Spanish web, hammock, and chandelier; performed as an acrobat on the Russian swing; and walked stilts in numerous shows and parades. In the summer of 2024, she spent two weeks with Outward Bound living in an Indigenous village in Panama, learning to scuba dive, kayaking for miles, and helping with sea turtle conservation—a trip that forever changed her perspective on life. She is currently pursuing her love of science and leadership at FGCU. When not actively leading or socializing, she can be found cheering on the FGCU basketball team, reading outdoors, or enjoying a coffee at her favorite local café.

KEPLER HENRY is sixteen years old and a junior in high school. He is an entrepreneur and artist at heart—with a passion for drawing—and has enjoyed growing his skills through the PreCollege immersion program at Ringling College of Art + Design. Kepler has lots of ideas for his career, many of which include living in a cabin in the woods, but also knows he has plenty of time to figure out what he wants to do with his life. For now, he is enjoying driving his Jeep around town and being sixteen.

He is a member of the elite Red Troupe of the Sailor Circus Academy in Sarasota, Florida, where he performs as a clown, unicyclist, and acrobat on the Russian swing. Kepler is an adrenaline seeker and is looking forward to bungee jumping and learning how to perform on the Wheel of Death in the circus as soon as possible. When he is not actively seeking his latest thrill, he can be found outdoors in the nearest hammock.